W9-BKB-692

BACK TO FULL EMPLOYMENT

BACK TO FULL EMPLOYMENT

Robert Pollin

A Boston Review Book

THE MIT PRESS Cambridge, Mass. London, England

MIT Press books may be purchased at special quantity discounts
for business or sales promotional use. For information, please
email special_sales@mitpress.mit.edu or write to Special Sales
Department, The MIT Press, 55 Hayward Street, Cambridge, MA
02142.

This book was set in Adobe Garamond by *Boston Review*
and was printed and bound in the United States of America.

Library of Congress Cataloging-in-Publication Data

Pollin, Robert.
Back to full employment / Robert Pollin.
    p.   cm. — (A Boston review book)
Includes bibliographical references and index.
ISBN 978-0-262-01757-2 (hardcover : alk. paper)
1. Full employment policies—United States. 2. United States—
Economic policy—2009– 3. Full employment policies. I.
Title.
HD5724.P573   2012
331.12'0424—dc23

2012013565

10   9   8   7   6   5   4   3   2   1

For Ruth Margalit Pollin-Galay
and Abe Pollin, in memory

CONTENTS

ACKNOWLEDGEMENTS

My first debt of gratitude is to Deb Chasman, the outstanding coeditor of the *Boston Review*. It was Deb's idea to produce a *Boston Review* Forum on the topic of full employment, building from some of my earlier and ongoing work. The forum came out in the January/February 2011 *BR*. Deb then proposed that an expanded version of my Forum article might work as a short book and took it upon herself to make this happen with MIT Press. The result is in your hands. Deb's editing associate at *BR* Simon Waxman also made many editing suggestions that improved the book.

In expanding the *BR* article, I have drawn on several of my other recent articles and studies of various sorts, many of which are listed in the references.

Some of these were first written for general readers in my regular "Economic Prospects" column with *New Labor Forum*. All of these columns benefitted greatly from my exchanges with Steve Fraser, the outstanding coeditor of *NLF*.

Two early incarnations of this material were initially presented as memorial lectures, honoring on separate occasions the life's work of David M. Gordon of the New School for Social Research and Sumner M. Rosen of Columbia University. Both Professors Gordon and Rosen, in their own ways, made major contributions in their lifetimes to advancing the causes of full employment and economic justice in the United States. I learned a great deal from the opportunity to reflect on their examples. I also benefitted from the comments by Gar Alperovitz, Helen Ginsberg, and Tom Weisskopf on my Rosen memorial lecture.

I am always learning from my interactions with graduate students, faculty members and other coworkers at the Economics Department and Political

Economy Research Institute (PERI) at my home institution, the University of Massachusetts-Amherst. There is not a more lively or challenging place to try to make oneself useful in addressing the most pressing economic problems of our time. Much of the material in this book builds in particular from my collaborations with fellow PERI researchers Jerry Epstein, Heidi Garrett-Peltier, James Heintz, Jeff Thompson, and Jeannette Wicks-Lim. I am deeply grateful to all of them, as well as to Judy Fogg and Debbie Zeidenberg, who somehow manage to keep PERI going.

I rely on the love and support of my mother, Irene Pollin and draw inspiration from the memory of my father, Abe Pollin. A taxi driver in Tel Aviv, Israel once explained to me that "children are investments, grandchildren are dividends." Being around Hannah, Asaf, and Ruthie Pollin-Galay convinces me that I have made some spectacular investments along the way. My wife, Sigrid Miller Pollin, and I have been discussing economics, social justice, the state of the world, and a whole lot more since we met during my first semester as a graduate student in 1975. My economics work is definitely several notches better because of her, and everything else is much better still.

1

*The Centrality of
Full Employment*

IN THE AFTERMATH OF THE 2008–09 WALL STREET collapse and worldwide Great Recession, employment conditions in the United States have been disastrous, worse than at any time since the 1930s Depression. Over the first three full years since Barack Obama entered office in January 2009, the official unemployment rate averaged 9.0 percent, representing nearly 14 million people in a labor force of about 153 million. By a broader definition, which includes people employed fewer hours than they would like and those discouraged from looking for work, the Labor Department calculates that the unemployment rate has averaged almost twice that amount, 16.5 percent between January 2009 and December 2011. This is more than 25 million people, a figure greater than the combined populations of the ten largest cities in the United States—New York, Los Angeles. Chicago, Houston, Phoenix, Philadelphia, San Antonio, San Diego, Dallas, and San Jose.

The first major act of the Obama administration was the economic stimulus program—the American Recovery and Reinvestment Act—focused precisely on counteracting the effects of the financial crisis and recession that had begun under George W. Bush. This $787 billion program of tax cuts and new government spending measures aimed to brace the economy's rickety floor, thereby preserving existing jobs and generating new ones in both the public and private sectors. The stimulus program did succeed in preventing a full-scale 1930s-style depression. But it has clearly proven inadequate for fully reversing the effects of the Wall Street collapse. Combined with the huge decline in tax revenues tied to the recession, the stimulus spending has also generated federal government fiscal deficits of a magnitude the United

States hasn't seen since World War II—around $1.4 trillion, or 10 percent of GDP in 2009, and around $1.3 trillion in 2010 and 2011, which was close to 9 percent of GDP in those years. It will clearly be a long, hard struggle to bring the U.S. economy, along with most of the rest of the world, out of the deep ditch into which Wall Street has shoved it.

New rounds of major job-generating measures—both government spending programs and, equally important, financial-market regulations and incentives to discourage hyper-speculative practices in favor of financing high-employment productive investments—are crucial to reversing the recession and driving down unemployment. Such measures will certainly fly in the face of the rising mantra in Washington, D.C. and throughout Europe in favor of fiscal austerity and business deregulation.

But beyond the challenges in advancing such short-term programs, there is a broader goal that is not even on the agenda. This goal is to push the U.S. economy toward full employment in the short run—i.e., over the next two to three years—and then sustain a full employment economy over the longer term. Especially at this historical juncture, as we attempt to grope our way out of the Great Recession and onto some kind of new growth trajectory, we need to be clear on the centrality of full employment as a policy goal. That is, we need to be focused on what exactly we mean by full employment and on why, properly defined, full employment is so fundamental to building a decent society. We then need to examine what kind of policy innovations, in both the short- and long-term, will be needed to get the United States economy to full employment and, once there, to stay there. These are the questions that I pursue in this short book.

Why Full Employment?

We can answer this both at the level of the individual and families; and in evaluating the health of an economy as a whole. Equally, as we will see later, creating a full employment economy can be joined effectively with another fundamental policy aim, which is to end our dependence on fossil fuels and create an economy powered by clean energy. On this matter we actually have no choice, assuming we want to stop playing Russian roulette with our environment.

Beginning with the individual's standpoint, whether you can get a job and, if so, whether the job offers decent pay and benefits, a clean and safe environment, and fair treatment for you and your coworkers, matters a lot to almost everyone. Money is the most obvious consideration. But beyond the money you earn, your job is also crucial for establishing your sense of security and self-worth, your health and safety, your ability to raise a family, and your chances to participate in the life of your community.

An abundance of job opportunities is also crucial to an economy's overall health. As employment levels rise, so does total purchasing power in the economy, since people have more money in their pockets to spend. This means more buoyant markets, greater business opportunities for both small and large firms, and strong incentives for private businesses to increase their level of investment. An economy with an abundance of decent jobs will also promote both individual opportunity and equality, because this kind of economy offers everyone the chance to provide for themselves and their families.

For these reasons, a high-employment economy is also the best single tool for fighting poverty. We saw this vividly in the United States from the late 1960s to 1970, when, as a result of the stimulus from both the Kennedy-Johnson tax cut and the buildup of Vietnam-related government spending, unemployment fell below 4 percent. This high-employment economy brought rising wages across the board, better working conditions, and less job discrimination against women, African Americans, and other minorities.

As such, full employment is also the most promising policy for fostering social and economic equality. As the Occupy Wall Street movement powerfully reminded everyone, income and wealth inequality have been rising in the United States for more than

30 years, most especially in the period just before the Wall Street crash. Thus, by the end of World War II, in 1946, the highest-income families—the top 1 percent—obtained 13 percent of all income and the top 10 percent obtained 37 percent. By the mid-1970s, the share of the top 10 percent had fallen to 33 percent of total income. However, beginning in the early 1980s, with the election of Ronald Reagan as President, this trend toward increasing income equality reversed itself. By 2007, just as the economic crisis was emerging, the top 1 percent's share of total income had risen to 24 percent—two-and-a-half times its share in 1970. The top 10 percent received 50 percent of all income, seventeen percentage points more than in 1970.[1] Unless people can count on getting hired into stable, decently paying jobs in the aftermath of the Great Recession, there is simply no way for them to receive the rising incomes that will be the basis for reversing this worsening pattern of inequality.

An economy operating at full employment evidently has the capacity to deliver great individual and social benefits. Why then doesn't everybody agree that this should be a fundamental goal of public policy, with debates focused on the narrower question of the most effective means of achieving this end?

In fact, coming out the 1930s Depression and World War II, creating full employment conditions was the central focus of economic policy throughout the world. Of course, the level of commitment to this goal varied substantially according to country and political parties in power. But it took the high inflation period of the 1970s and subsequent neoliberal revolution—marked most decisively by the elections of Margaret Thatcher as U.K. Prime Minister in 1979 and Ronald Reagan as U.S. President in 1980—to supplant full employment as the centerpiece of economic policy in favor of a framework most amenable to Wall Street and global capitalists. This shift included macroeconomic policies focused on maintaining low inflation rather than full employment; reducing the public sector, including welfare state programs; eliminating or weakening pro-worker labor laws; eliminating barriers to international trade; and of course deregulating financial markets. It was the neoliberal commitment to financial deregulation in particular that proved to be the most direct cause of the Wall Street collapse and Great Recession.

Coming out of the Great Recession, the challenge before us now is to create a new, workable full employment policy framework as a serious alternative to what increasingly appears the prevailing approach, which is to patch up and restart the failed neoliberal model.

What We Mean by Full Employment

Defining full employment is a much more difficult question than one might imagine. This point was pounded into me when I was working in Bolivia in 1990 as part of a UN-commissioned economic advising team led by Keith Griffin of University of California, Riverside. Griffin's assignment was to develop a program that would address the human devastation wrought by the "shock therapy" program designed by Professor Jeffrey Sachs to end the Bolivian hyperinflation of the 1980s. This was one variant of neoliberalism as applied in developing countries, consisting of massive cuts in government spending and public sector layoffs.

Griffin asked me to examine employment policies, so I paid a visit to the economists at the Ministry of Planning. When I suggested that we discuss the country's unemployment problem, they explained that the country had no unemployment problem. I asked about the people begging, shining shoes, or hawking batteries and Chiclets in the street just below the window where we stood. They responded that those people *were* employed.

The lesson was clear. In Bolivia then, just as in the United States today, we have to pose the question of full employment more precisely. It is not simply a matter of everyone spending their days trying to scratch out a living somehow. A workable definition of full employment should refer to an abundance of *decent jobs*.

But this then raises the question: what is a decent job? While it is difficult to pin this down in terms of dollars and cents, Lawrence Glickman captured well the essence of the idea in his history of living wage movements in the United States from the nineteenth century onward, *A Living Wage: American Workers and the Making of Consumer Society* (1999). Glickman defined a living wage job as being one that pays "a wage level that offers workers the ability to support families, to maintain self-respect, and to have both the means and the leisure to participate in the civic life of the nation" (p. 3). In addition to paying living wages, the standards for a decent job must also include workplaces that are safe and healthy. Either as members of unions or by other means, workers also need to be able to participate meaningfully in the decisions that affect their working lives. Taking account of all these various factors, a policy of full employment at decent jobs is thus most certainly a challenge to the prerogatives of capitalists and the logic of neoliberalism. How much of a challenge is the question to which we turn next.

2

*Is Full Employment Possible
Under Capitalism?*

IN SEEKING TO ANSWER THE QUESTION POSED IN this chapter's title, we should begin by defining three distinct types of unemployment. *Voluntary* unemployment occurs when people are out of work because they choose to be. *Frictional* unemployment occurs when people are between jobs, receiving job training, or relocating. *Involuntary* unemployment occurs when people are making a significant effort to find work, but have been unsuccessful. In principle, the first two types of unemployment are relatively benign. Unemployment only becomes a serious concern when it is involuntary. But as we will see, the distinctions between the three categories are not always evident.

Marx and Keynes: Setting the Terms of Debate

The first major theorist of unemployment was Karl Marx, who addressed the issue at great length in the first volume of his 1867 magnum opus *Capital*, especially in his justly famous Chapter 25, "The General Law of Capitalist Accumulation."

One of Marx's overarching themes was that, in a free market capitalist economy, workers will generally have less power than capitalists in the bargaining process over wages. This is because workers cannot fall back on other means of staying alive if they fail to get hired into a job. Capitalists gain higher profits through having this relatively stronger bargaining position. But Marx also stressed that workers' bargaining power diminishes further when (involuntary) unemployment and underemployment are high, since that means that employed workers can be more readily replaced by what he called "the reserve army" of the unemployed outside the office, mine, or factory gates.

Pursuing the implications of this observation, Marx concluded that high involuntary unemployment serves an essential function within the operations of a capitalist economy. By the same token, when a capitalist economy is growing rapidly enough to deplete the reserve army, workers will then utilize their increased bargaining power to raise wages and shift the distribution of income in their favor. Profits are correspondingly squeezed. As a result, capitalists become less willing to risk spending money on new investment projects. This then leads to a fall in job creation, higher unemployment, and a replenishment of the reserve army. In other words, the reserve army of unemployed is the instrument capitalists use to prevent significant wage increases and thereby maintain profitability.

John Maynard Keynes was the next great theorist on the issue of unemployment. Keynes developed his arguments in the midst of the 1930s Great Depression, most forcefully in his own 1936 magnum opus, *The General Theory of Employment, Interest, and Money*. Like Marx, Keynes understood clearly that the operations of capitalist economies could easily generate mass involuntary unemployment. Keynes also fully understood, along with Marx, that mass unemployment was a social scourge. But Keynes departed from Marx by reaching the conclusion that mass unemployment was not, in fact, necessary to the operations of capitalism. Indeed, Keynes to this day is the most widely cited economist on the planet (with the possible exception of Marx) precisely because of the policy measures he developed for preventing mass unemployment and advancing a full employment agenda within the framework of capitalism.

For Keynes, mass unemployment resulted because of insufficiency in total spending—or aggregate demand—in the economy, including the total of household, private-investment, and government demand, as well as the total amount of export sales less total imports. According to Keynes, by far the most volatile type of spending in a capitalist economy is private investment. Decisions by businesses to invest depend on their expectations of future profits, what Keynes termed their "animal spirits." Animal spirits could fall for a number of reasons. One factor could be the dynamic described by Marx, in which wages could rise quickly as the reserve army becomes depleted, thereby squeezing profits. Another factor could be rising competition from imports. Still another possibility is the classic bursting of a financial market bubble, such as occurred in 2008–09. Whatever the immediate cause of capitalists' declining animal spirits, when they do fall, private investment will correspondingly contract. This, in turn, means that businesses will also be laying off workers, producing rising involuntary unemployment.

Keynes was convinced that the wise application of well-designed policies could counteract this inherent tendency, and thereby create and sustain full employment capitalism. The Keynesian approach was centered on macroeconomic policy. The first idea was that central governments could manipulate their spending levels—creating fiscal deficits or surpluses—to counteract fluctuations in private business spending. This is what is meant by activist "Keynesian" fiscal policies. The experience over 2008–09 was a prime example of such policies. That is, when private business spending falls sharply due to the collapse of a financial bubble, as occurred in 2008–09, it is then the government's responsibility to counteract this by increasing its own spending, borrowing money itself, and running fiscal deficits as needed, in order to support overall spending in the economy.

The Keynesian macroeconomic policy approach also includes adjusting interest rates and the availability of credit—i.e., monetary policy—to maintain the economy's overall level of demand. Here again the United States Federal Reserve's current policy of holding its target interest rate at nearly zero percent for three years as a means of encouraging borrowing and spending is another prime example of activist monetary policies inspired by Keynesian principles.

The third major element of the Keynesian policy toolkit is financial regulation. If, as Keynes held, the major cause of economic instability and mass unemployment under capitalism is the volatility of private business investment, then allowing financial market players, on Wall Street and elsewhere, to operate without regulations would inevitably lead to excessive speculation and financial bubbles. This is what Keynes himself observed during the 1920s and 1930s. Obviously this pattern repeated itself during the most recent financial bubble and collapse.

It was largely under the influence of Keynes's arguments from the end of World War II until the early 1970s that economic policies in the capitalist societies were targeted to achieving full employment. To be sure, the level of commitment to this goal varied substantially according to country and political party, as did the specific policy approaches for maintaining a high level of overall demand. But nevertheless, the idea of running economies at something approximating full employment, and utilizing macroeconomic policy tools and financial regulations to make this happen, was almost universally a front-and-center concern.

Friedman and Kalecki: New Syntheses and Explosive Conclusions

It is no small irony that Keynesian policies were embraced so strongly immediately after the 2008–09 crisis. This is because Keynes's approach had fallen out of favor three decades earlier and was almost entirely supplanted by neoliberalism from the late 1970s onward.

One major precept of neoliberalism is that government policies to promote full employment are doomed to failure and that free market policies are themselves the most effective means for producing the fairest possible employment conditions for everyone. The most powerful voice in advancing this perspective was the late University of Chicago economist Milton Friedman, who originated the term "natural rate of unemployment" in his highly influential presidential address to the American Economic Association in 1967.

In reading this lecture by Friedman, one finds an unlikely parallel between his ideas and those of Marx.

This is because Friedman, like Marx, held that high unemployment in capitalist economies occurs when workers have the capacity to flex their bargaining muscles. Friedman's reasoning is as follows: if we allow for free and competitive markets, businesses will always be forced to hire a worker at a wage exactly equal to the amount of money that this worker is worth to the business. If businesses try to hire workers at a wage lower than what they are worth, the business will not be able to attract qualified employees and will be outcompeted by businesses that are willing to pay workers a fair wage. By the same token, if businesses pay workers more than they are worth, the businesses will see their profits disappear, and, again, will eventually fold.

This is how Friedman concludes that free market capitalism will ensure that businesses are offering workers jobs at an appropriate wage. Workers are "free to choose" in Friedman's framework: to accept a job at this appropriate wage, or not to work. If workers freely decide not to work at the wage offered, they are, according to Friedman, *voluntarily* unemployed. In Friedman's terminology, the "natural rate" of *involuntary* unemployment in a free market setting is effectively zero (after allowing for such "frictions" as people moving between jobs and acquiring new skills). The natural rate of involuntary unemployment will become positive only when workers refuse to accept this free market–determined wage or when non-market forces, such as labor unions or minimum wage mandates, prevent wage levels from falling to the level that is consistent with business profitability. Here is how Friedman put it in his 1967 lecture:

> By using the term 'natural' rate of unemployment, I do not mean to suggest that it is immutable and unchangeable. On the contrary, many of the market characteristics that determine its level are man-made and policy-made. In the United States, for example, legal minimum wage rates . . . and the strength of labor unions all make the natural rate of unemployment higher than it would otherwise be. (1968, p. 9)

The final major thinker on unemployment that we need to consider is Michal Kalecki, a Polish socialist who was a contemporary of Keynes and who tried to synthesize the perspectives of Marx along with Keynes. In his classic 1943 paper "Political Aspects of Full Employment," Kalecki reasoned as follows:

Due to Keynes, we now have a sufficient understanding of capitalist economies such that we can devise workable policies to sustain full employment. Moreover, contrary to Marx, Kalecki held that full employment can be beneficial to profits, because the economy will be operating with buoyant markets, at a high level of overall demand for products. Business profits could well be squeezed by high wage demands in a full employment economy, but they could compensate through a higher volume of sales combined with smaller, but still positive, profit margins.

Despite the fact that businesses could benefit from full employment in this way, Kalecki reasoned that they still would not support full employment as a goal because it would embolden workers excessively. Full employment could threaten the capitalists' control over the workplace, the pace and direction of economic activity, and even a society's political institutions.

These arguments led Kalecki to some striking conclusions. He did first recognize that full employment was theoretically achievable under capitalism by applying Keynesian policy measures. But, for Kalecki, the Keynesian approach was too narrowly technical, since Keynes did not take into consideration the fact that full employment would challenge the capitalists' social and political hegemony. For Kalecki then, full employment under capitalism could succeed only if these social and political forces could be contained, regardless of how well Keynesian macroeconomic policies could be implemented in technical terms. From this perspective, Kalecki held that fascism, which he deplored, could nevertheless be an effective framework for operating full employment capitalism. This is because the job of a fascist government would be to maintain the capitalists' control over workers, no matter whether the workers had jobs or not. Whether or not Kalecki was correct, he underscored dramatically the social and political challenges tied to building a full employment economy.

Inflation, Unemployment and the Swedish Model
The Swedes developed the most effective answer to date to Kalecki's challenge—a policy framework *other than fascism* that can manage the inevitable conflicts between workers and capitalists that emerge in a full employment economy. Their success turned on an answer to the most common argument against trying to operate an economy at full employment: the fear of excessive inflation.

In 1958 the British economist A.W. Phillips observed a long-term relationship between unemployment and inflation: inflation goes up when unemployment goes down, and vice versa. This relationship has come to be known as the Phillips Curve. The logic behind the Phillips Curve follows readily from Marx's idea that workers are able to bargain up wages when unemployment is low, causing profits to fall, which in turn means less business investment and a new round of rising unemployment. But unlike Marx, who saw lower profits as an inevitable result of high employment, Phillips suggested that business profits need not be squeezed by high employment. Rather, businesses could pass on higher labor costs to customers through price increases, causing a wage-price spiral, i.e. continuing inflation.

Indeed, it was the failure of the advanced capitalist economies—in North America, Western Europe, and Japan—to contain inflation in the 1970s that allowed the full-employment policy goal to be eclipsed by Friedman's "natural rate of unemployment" theory. Economic policymakers worldwide became convinced that inflation resulting from low unemployment had become severe and uncontrollable.

In fact, this global march toward Friedmanite economics misread the primary cause of high inflation in the 1970s, which was not low unemployment, but the two oil price shocks—the threefold jump in

1973–74 and a similar spike in 1979. Nonetheless, addressing the issue of inflation control in building a full employment economy is a crucial challenge.

Sweden managed to meet this challenge successfully for three decades, due to the model developed by economists Rudolf Meidner and Gösta Rehn.[1] Meidner and Rehn did support macroeconomic policies to stimulate overall demand in the economy and thereby expand the number of decent-paying jobs. But they understood that unacceptably high inflation could result if stimulus measures alone aimed to bring the economy all the way to zero involuntary employment. So they also favored limiting such policy interventions, targeting, through these measures, an unemployment rate of about three percent. They believed some slack in the economy would keep upward wage pressure from producing headlong inflation.[2]

Alongside restraints on job stimulus policies, Meidner and Rehn then also supported the government's active labor market interventions to help as many as possible of the remaining unemployed workers into jobs. These interventions included travel and relocation allowances, retraining programs, and other measures targeted at mopping up frictional unemployment.

As this Swedish policy developed in practice, it operated with the cooperation of working people and their union representatives. Sweden's main unions accepted restrictions on macroeconomic stimulus policies and their own wage bargaining demands in order to help fight excessive inflationary pressures as full employment approached. Sweden thus succeeded at maintaining unemployment at an average rate of 2.1 percent between 1960 and 1989. Inflation averaged a fairly high 6.7 percent, but this period includes the effects of the 1970s, when inflation and unemployment rose together due to the two oil price shocks, not a tight labor market. The effects of the oil price shocks no doubt undermined the effectiveness of this approach, but the model worked over a long time period because of the unions' restraint in wage bargaining on behalf of maintaining full employment.

Of course, this approach could not be transplanted intact into the current U.S. economy, since today's U.S. labor movement is far less powerful than the Swedish movement of the 1960s–1970s. But the lessons from Sweden for the U.S. labor movement are more about general principles than specific historical conditions. Thus, the U.S. labor movement should take it upon itself to design a workable full employment program today, recognizing in that program the importance of inflation control as full employment is approached. The unions should be specific as to how they themselves could be major contributors to achieving and maintaining full employment with low inflation, building in relevant ways from the Swedish model. Through such measures, the representatives of U.S. workers could bring significant new voices to the debate over inflation as well as employment, rather than giving free rein over the management of inflation to the Federal Reserve and Wall Street.

At the same time, the experience in Sweden poses additional challenges for the United States today. Despite their success, the Swedes largely abandoned their commitment to a full employment economy in the early 1990s, shifting their priority much more toward inflation control. Between 1993–2006, unemployment rose to an average of 7.6 percent, while inflation fell sharply, to an average of 1.5 percent. Helen Ginsburg and Marguirite Rosenthal attribute the shift to "the growing power of Swedish business, pressures from globalization and the race to join the European Union, with its requirements for low budget deficits and inflation but none for low unemployment" (2006, p. 1).[3] The Swedish experience thus raises the question as to whether the model has become unworkable in our contemporary globalized economy. This is the issue we consider next.

3

Globalization, Immigration, and Trade

IN EXAMINING THE EFFECTS OF GLOBALIZATION on the viability of full employment policies in the United States, Sweden, or anywhere else, the most relevant concern is not the pattern of increasing economic interconnectedness between countries per se. It is rather the neoliberal policy framework that has defined the process of globalization for the past 35 years.

In the U.S. labor market, the neoliberal policy framework has exposed working people to increased competition from workers in poor countries—it has meant, effectively, an expansion of the reserve army of labor for the jobs done by U.S. workers, despite the fact that not all products on U.S. markets are imported from poor countries, nor are U.S. firms moving their operations offshore. The domestic U.S. economy remains a $15 trillion operation, employing 140 million people. But U.S. workers nevertheless face an increasingly *credible threat* that they can be supplanted by workers in poor countries willing to accept much lower wages. Employers can tell workers: "If you won't accept a pay cut, we'll move." Or "If you want a union, fine. We'll start buying what you make from China."[1]

The trend for average wages since the early 1970s suggests the seriousness of this problem. In 2011 the average non-supervisory worker in the United States earned $19.47 an hour (in 2011 dollars). This figure is 7 percent below the 1972 peak of $20.99 per hour (also in 2011 dollars). The long-term pattern for health and other benefits has broadly followed that for wages, so that total compensation for U.S. workers—including both wages and benefits—has stagnated for 40 years. But this is only half the story. While wages fell, average labor productivity in the United States rose by 111 percent. That is, the total basket of goods and services that average U.S. workers produced in 2011 is more than double what they could manage in 1972. Their reward has been a 7 percent pay cut. Figure 1 portrays this movement for average wages and productivity vividly.

Figure 1. Average Real Wages and Productivity Level in the United States, 1960 - 2011

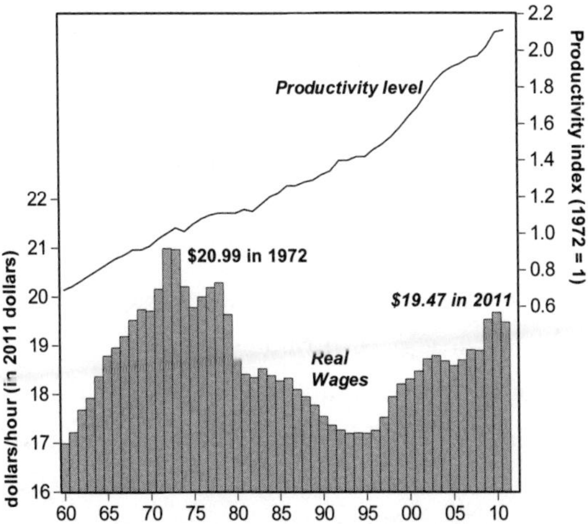

Source: U.S. Bureau of Labor Statistics
Note: Productivity index measures output per hour of all persons in private business.
Wages are median hourly earnings in 2011 dollars for nonsupervisory private sector workers.

This combination of falling real wages and rising productivity is, in turn, a primary contributor to rising U.S. inequality over the past 30 years. If workers have not been receiving the financial benefits from their own rising productivity, then those benefits have to be flowing elsewhere. Specifically, they are flowing upwards, to the people who own businesses, either directly or through their portfolios of financial market investments.

Unless our policy environment changes dramatically, the threat effects from globalization are likely to only deepen. This point was brought home by an unlikely source, a 2006 article in *Foreign Affairs*, the longtime premier organ of the country's foreign policy elite. In this article, Alan Blinder—former member of President Clinton's Council of Economic Advisors and a former Vice-Chair of the Federal Reserve Board under Alan Greenspan—suggests that something like 20–30 percent of all U.S. jobs can be performed by workers in poor countries. This amounts to about 30–40 million jobs in total in today's labor market.

Blinder includes all manufacturing jobs as well as what he calls "impersonal service" jobs. These refer to services that can be delivered over the Internet, such as back office accountants, lawyers, engineers, architects, and laboratory technicians, as well as their support staff. This doesn't mean that anything like 40 million jobs will actually be outsourced. The point is that the employers of these 40 million workers will gain leverage over their workers because their power to make credible threats to outsource will grow.

In designing full employment policies to counteract these pressures from neoliberal globalization, the U.S. experience in the late 1990s provides an important reference point. As unemployment fell below four percent in this period for the first time since 1969, the long-term decline in wages temporarily reversed itself. Workers attained better health and pension benefits. The poverty rate declined. The patterns we observed in the 1960s quickly began to reassert themselves, even in the face of globalization pressures pushing in the other direction.

The problem with the 1990s, however, is that the rapid economic growth that drove unemployment down was spurred by an overheated speculative stock market, similar to the most recent financial bubble led by the real estate market. The 1990s financial bubble created a large-scale injection of new spending into the U.S. economy, as wealthy people borrowed unprecedented amounts of money for consumption and investment. But this financial bubble, as with all such bubbles, proved to be unsustainable. When it collapsed in early 2001, well before the September 11th attack, recession followed. The rise in average real wages ended soon thereafter. There has not been any sustained improvement in real wages since.

Avoiding Bad Alternatives to Neoliberalism

But recognizing that neoliberal policies, not globalization per se, are the real threat to U.S. workers' living standards does not mean that any and all alternatives to neoliberalism will make life better for U.S. workers. In fact, over the past few years, two alternatives to neoliberal globalization policies have emerged forcefully within mainstream and even some progressive policy circles in the U.S. These are 1) restricting immigration into the U.S. and thereby helping preserve jobs in the U.S. for native workers; and 2) pursuing a more aggressive nationalistic stance on international trade, in order to expand U.S. export markets and limit imports. However, as we will see, neither of these approaches will deliver significant benefits for U.S. workers. Equally important, these approaches also miss what should be a guiding principle of any desirable alternative to neoliberalism. This is to create an abundance of decent jobs in all countries, as opposed to trying to improve conditions for native U.S. workers at the expense of either U.S. immigrants or those in other countries.

Can We Please Stop Blaming Immigrants?[2]
With the Wall Street collapse and Great Recession generating mass unemployment, hostility in the United States toward immigrants has risen sharply.

The strongest sign of this growing animosity was the law signed in April 2010 by Arizona Governor Jan Brewer, which gave police broad powers to detain anyone suspected of being an illegal immigrant. A few months later, two U.S. Senators, Jon Kyl of Arizona and Lindsey Graham of South Carolina, tried to push the point still further by calling for the repeal of the Fourteenth Amendment to the U.S. Constitution. The Fourteenth Amendment grants automatic citizenship to all babies born on U.S. soil, regardless of the citizenship status of the baby's parents.

But while the pressures on U.S. workers of neoliberal globalization are real and longstanding, they are also distinct in their effects from the basic fact that lots of immigrants are living and working in the United States, some of them illegally. Immigration into the United States has been rising steadily since the 1970s, after having fallen for 60 years from its peak level around 1910. At present, immigrant arrivals—running at about 1.25 million people per year—account for 40 percent of population growth nationally, and a much larger share in some regions. Something like 35–40 percent of new arrivals are undocumented immigrants from Mexico and Central America with low education and limited English skills.

The logic that leads people to blame immigrants for mass unemployment seems straightforward. Let's assume that, at any given time, there are a fixed number of jobs available. If immigrants take a significant share of the available jobs at low wages, that will mean fewer jobs are available for U.S. natives. The increased competition for the given number of jobs will also weaken workers' bargaining power and thus drive wages down.

But does this simple logic accurately describe what is really happening out in the world? In fact, after decades of debate, including studies by researchers from a wide range of disciplines and political persuasions, the weight of evidence strongly supports the conclusion that immigrants—including undocumented workers—are not, on balance, hurting job opportunities or wages for native U.S. workers.

Some of the most innovative research on the jobs question has been done by the U.C. Berkeley economist David Card.[3] Focusing on data from the 2000 census, Card compared local labor market conditions in the seventeen largest metropolitan areas throughout the United States.

There were two reasons that Card made this comparison. First, large numbers of immigrants live in these cities, comprising, on average nearly 27 percent of their populations. That is roughly twice their share of the country as a whole. So if immigration is having a substantial effect on jobs anywhere in the United States, we should be able to see it most clearly in these large cities. Second, the percentage of immigrants varies dramatically *between* these different cities. Philadelphia and Detroit are at the low end, with immigrants accounting for 8 percent of their total populations, while the figure is 35 percent in Los Angeles and Miami. If immigrants are indeed making conditions more difficult for native workers, we would therefore expect that native workers will be worse off in places like Los Angeles than Philadelphia, after we control for other factors affecting the labor markets in these cities, such as the relative levels of business investment, changes in population, or the overall unemployment rate.

In particular, we would expect the pressures of competition with immigrant workers to be felt most acutely by those with low educational credentials, such as restaurant workers, hotel workers, taxi drivers, cleaning people, practical nurses, and gardeners. Since immigrants tend to have less formal education than native workers, they would be more active in competing for these types of jobs. However, Card showed that there are no significant differences from city to city in terms of either numbers of jobs available or wage levels for native workers, regardless of the proportion of immigrants living in the city. Other researchers have reached basically the same conclusion, using different methodologies and data.

But skeptics nevertheless raise the issue: Why hasn't the increased immigrant population forced down job opportunities and wages for low-credentialed natives? If economists cling to any core precepts in their thinking, the first has to be the law of supply and demand. This includes the idea that if the supply of something goes up while demand stays the same, prices will fall, and some of the excess supply will likely go unsold. If we are talking about immigrants increasing the overall supply of workers looking for jobs, their impact within this supply and demand logic should be to deliver lower wages (price of labor falling) and more unemployment (workers unable to sell their labor services to businesses). Thus, without repealing the simple logic of supply and demand, how is it possible that a rising supply of immigrant workers in the United States does not cause lower wages and higher unemployment?

As many researchers have shown, one key factor is that immigrants do not just increase the supply of labor, but also increase overall market demand.[4] Immigrants living in the United States buy consumer goods and cars in this country, and they either own or rent homes. These purchases create more buoyant U.S. markets. This in turn encourages businesses to invest more and hire more workers. In addition, immigrants start their own businesses at a higher rate than native U.S. residents. This raises demand for business-related supplies, such as computers and office furniture, and services such as bookkeeping, accounting, and legal counsel. Indeed, the large immigrant populations of Los Angeles, Miami, New York, and elsewhere have also drawn foreign investment into these cities. All of these factors also help support wage rates at least at the levels they would be in the absence of the increased levels of market demand created by immigrants.

Jeannette Wicks-Lim and I (2011) have recently updated this research and found that these same results have held up over the 2008–09 recession. An important additional factor in the recession years is that immigration rates vary with the economy's overall cyclical swings. The recession has thus led to an accelerated rate of reverse migration: immigrants returning to their home countries precisely because opportunities in the United States have declined.

Despite these broad findings, there are still conditions in which high levels of in-migration can generate negative economic effects. As a prime example, the situation with farm workers is a clear case in which large numbers of immigrants seeking jobs—including a high percentage of undocumented workers—do push down wages for everyone in agriculture.[5] However, this situation is unique because the total number of people employed as agricultural workers is too small—at only 6.5 percent of just rural employment—to affect overall economic conditions within any given region. As a more general case, if there were an extremely rapid increase in the urban immigrant population, combined with a sharp slowdown in the rate of out-migration, this could reduce job opportunities and wages for natives, especially those looking for work at the low end of the wage scale. But this combination of events has not happened to date, even amid the ongoing economic slump.

The Limits of Trade Nationalism[6]

Another outgrowth of the ongoing U.S. employment crisis has been rising demands across the United States political spectrum for the United States to become more aggressive about closing the roughly $700 billion annual gap between the imports we purchase and the exports we sell on global markets. This is certainly an issue worth exploring. That is, how much, by itself, could a change in our global trade policies—including especially tariff restrictions on imports or lowering the value of the dollar relative to other currencies—accomplish toward pushing the unemployment rate down significantly? My own answer is: not very much. At the same time, Buy America provisions can sometimes, but not always, make sense, as one part of a broader set of industrial policies, especially on behalf of building a clean-energy economy. More generally, the issues at play entail several twists and turns, at times involving a most undesirable situation of pitting the well-being of U.S. workers against those in other countries.

Tariffs and dollar depreciation are weak policy tools.
The United States has been importing more than it exports for 35 straight years. In 2007, just before the Wall Street collapse and recession, the trade deficit amounted to 5.8 percent of GDP. During the 2008–09 recession, the trade deficit did fall along with overall spending both in the U.S. and throughout the world, though, as of 2009, the deficit still amounted to a substantial 3.6 percent of GDP. Let's say the U.S could reduce its imports by 10 percent and increase its exports by the same amount. Those changes by themselves would generate roughly four million new jobs in the United States, a bit more than 20 percent of the total needed to bring the economy to around 4 percent unemployment in today's economy. A high proportion of these new jobs generated by reducing our trade deficit would be in manufacturing, thus delivering major benefits to the hard-hit major manufacturing regions of the country, such as Ohio and Michigan.

These are impressive numbers, more than sufficient to persuade a large number of analysts, including many progressive economists, to think that we could indeed deliver substantial employment benefits in the United States through a shift in our trade policies. One approach would be simply to impose new tariffs on imports coming into the United States. This would increase the prices of imported goods in the United States, making them less attractive to consumers. Another would be to lower the value of the dollar by, say, 20 percent relative to the euro, Japanese yen, and Chinese yuan. Assuming this could be accomplished, the cheaper dollar would mean that the prices of foreign-made goods would rise in the U.S. market, while the prices that foreigners would pay for U.S. products would fall. This should discourage U.S. imports and encourage exports.

However, in my view, neither raising tariffs nor lowering the value of the dollar, on their own, is likely to produce any significant job gains for workers in the United States, either in the short or long run. What are the problems with imposing tariffs and lowering the value of the dollar?

The issue is more straightforward in the case of tariffs. Any such tariffs would have to be set relatively high, like the 10 percent surcharge imposed by President Nixon in 1971 in order to seriously discourage U.S. consumers and businesses from purchasing imports. But setting a high tariff barrier against foreign producers seeking access to U.S. markets would no doubt provoke other countries to retaliate, which in turn would reduce our exports as well as our imports. The net result could still be some gain in overall U.S. employment, since the U.S. market is larger than those of its trading partners. But in the face of foreign retaliation, the overall benefits would almost certainly be modest.

Lowering the value of the dollar is a less overtly aggressive act than imposing new tariffs. But it is not even clear that the United States could keep the dollar at a significantly lower level on a sustained basis, even if the Europeans, Japanese, and Chinese did not retaliate. The ongoing economic crisis in Europe has pushed down the euro relative to the dollar, so global traders are clinging to their dollar-based assets, which in turn props up the value of the dollar in currency markets.

But even if we could succeed in lowering the dollar on a sustained basis, it still would not follow that our imports would fall and our exports would rise significantly. The evidence on this question is decidedly mixed. In any case, the key to competing in the high-end manufacturing industry that will be needed to, among other things, build a clean-energy economy over the next generation—including components for mass rail transit, wind turbines, and solar panels—is producing high-quality products, not modestly cheaper domestic versions of products made at higher quality levels elsewhere.

Moreover, maintaining a lower dollar will still not prevent foreign competitors from outcompeting U.S. producers on price itself. Consider now lower-end products, such as garments and textiles, and the situation for businesses in developing countries seeking to export these products into the United States.

When a fall in the dollar stiffens price competition for exporters in developing countries, they will likely respond by lowering their own costs and prices to remain competitive. They could do this either by increasing productivity in their factories or by cutting their workers' wages. Here, then, is one major instance where an aggressive U.S. trade stance can worsen conditions for workers in developing countries without even expanding employment in the United States.

This raises the more general point: let's say we can succeed in moving jobs from foreign countries to the U.S. Should we consider this an entirely desirable outcome, especially with respect to developing countries? As a long-term strategy, less developed countries should grow increasingly over time on the basis of expanding their domestic markets—i.e. with their own people earning wages high enough to be able to buy the products they themselves produce. This expansion of domestic markets will be a crucial result of a successful jobs expansion program in less developed economies, just as it is in the U.S. But this does not gainsay the fact that, at present, less developed economies can benefit greatly through selling products on the much larger markets in rich countries.

The United States can reach full employment with a trade deficit. It is important to recall that at the end of the Clinton presidency, we did in fact reach very low unemployment rates while operating with trade policies and a trade deficit similar to those in place today. For the last four months of 2000, unemployment fell below 4 percent for the first time in 40 years. The trade deficit during 2000 was 3.8 percent of GDP, roughly the same as 2009. It is true that the excellent employment trends in that period were driven by an unprecedented stock market bubble. But this experience only underscores a fundamental challenge: if we can create a growth engine for the United States economy other than some type of asset bubble, we demonstrably have the means to reach near-full employment even while carrying a large trade deficit.

Public investment and "Buy American." Public investments and industrial policies will have to play a critical role here. As I discuss in detail in Chapter 5, they can be a driving force pushing overall investment activity in the United States into productive projects such as building a clean-energy economy, as opposed to yet new variations on casino capitalism. Public investments entail creating a modernized infrastructure capable of lowering operating costs for business, while industrial policies can provide research and development support for technical innovations, cheap credit, tax benefits, and guaranteed markets. In combination, these measures will certainly enhance the global competitiveness of U.S. businesses.

In the context of such publicly funded investment activities, it is appropriate that the majority of spending and job creation be channeled into the communities in which the taxpayers themselves reside. This means that some form of regulations promoting purchases of domestically produced goods is justified in the context of a broader industrial policy and public investment agenda. For example, the "Buy American" standards that currently apply to government purchases of autos, buses, and trains require that 60 percent of the components be produced in the United States and that the assembly also be performed within the United States.

But how far to go with such standards cannot be determined by appeals to general principles—either that U.S. taxpayer-funded projects should *only* purchase U.S.-made products, or that publicly-funded projects should be free of any Buy America provisions. Unavoidably, we rather need to weigh conflicting considerations. For example, if U.S. industrial policies and public investments do succeed in delivering an effective infrastructure, cheap credit, tax benefits, and guaranteed markets to U.S. firms, this will certainly assist U.S. businesses to operate competitively relative to foreign producers. What if some U.S. businesses still are unable to compete against foreign producers, even after receiving these advantages from an effective U.S. industrial policy? Certainly at that point, these

U.S. firms should be allowed to fail, rather than be given further benefits to prop them up against foreign competitors.

The best way to make these issues less complicated is for the United States to commit to a set of policies capable of delivering full employment. If the United States successfully implemented full employment policies, then an important additional result would follow: an economy open to imports would be far less pain-inducing for U.S. workers. From the workers' standpoint, trade protectionist policies are actually a form of social protection. But trade protectionist measures are a poor substitute for direct forms of social protection, the most important of which is full employment.

A broader conclusion also emerges clearly. The real problem with U.S. employment conditions has never been globalization broadly defined, nor is it immigration or the trade deficit. We know from the late 1990s experience that we can reach full employment with rising wages even after allowing for current levels of global integration, immigration, and a trade deficit. The real problem is therefore the absence of a full employment agenda that takes account of the challenges presented by globalization, along with other major challenges. These are the issues to which we now turn, focusing on the short-term agenda in Chapter 4 and long-term policies in Chapter 5.

4

*Digging Out
of Recession*

AFTER WALL STREET HYPER-SPECULATION brought the global economy to its knees in 2008–09, economic policymakers throughout the world—including the United States, the countries of the European Union, Japan, South Korea, China, India, and Brazil—all enacted extraordinary measures to counteract the crisis.

In the United States, the first large-scale policy move was the notorious bailouts of the big banks, aimed at preventing them from collapsing altogether and thereby risking a 1930s-style depression. They also included Federal Reserve monetary policies that pushed the target short-term interest rate—the "federal funds rate" at which commercial banks can borrow —to near zero by mid-2008. As of this writing, the Fed has sustained the near-zero short-term rate for three-and-a-half years, and Federal Reserve Chair Ben Bernanke has stated his intention to continue this policy through 2014. The final major measure has been the fiscal stimulus, and the accompanying major expansion in the federal government's fiscal deficit. I will focus first on fiscal policies—the stimulus program and the federal deficit—because the issue of its success or failure has come to dominate economic policy discussions as we approach the 2012 election. Moreover, our discussions on monetary policy and the banking system will benefit from an introduction to the fiscal picture.

The Obama Fiscal Stimulus Program

Barack Obama signed the American Recovery and Reinvestment Act (ARRA) into law in February 2009. The bill, which included $787 billion in new government spending and tax cuts for households and businesses, was the first major act of Obama's presidency. As Obama's first term is reaching its end, the ARRA remains his most aggressive initiative to fight mass unemployment.

Meanwhile, the U.S. fiscal deficit grew rapidly starting in 2009. The deficit reached $1.4 trillion, or 10 percent of GDP that year, and $1.3 trillion in both 2010 and 2011, equal to 8.9 and 8.5 percent of GDP in those years. Prior to that, the deficit averaged 2 percent of GDP under George W. Bush (2001–08) and 0.8 percent of GDP under Bill Clinton (1993–2000).

Of course, the stimulus program deliberately aimed to increase the federal government's deficit. The goal was to inject needed spending into the economy, which could generate a virtuous cycle of falling unemployment, improving business conditions, and falling deficits as a result of rising incomes and tax revenues. At the same time, the federal deficit would have expanded in any case due to the recession. This is because, as a normal result of the recession, tax revenues flowing into the government fell along with incomes, business profits, and asset prices, while government payments for "automatic stabilizers"—such as unemployment insurance, Medicaid, and other basic safety nets—rose. In addition, even before the recession began, the federal tax cuts enacted in 2001 and 2003 under George W. Bush, which primarily benefited the wealthy, contributed significantly to enlarging the federal deficits every year.

Unemployment officially stood at 8.2 percent when the ARRA was enacted in February 2009. It rose to an average of around 9 percent in the three subsequent years. The fact that the stimulus program has not delivered a decline in unemployment has created a strong wave of opposition to this policy. Indeed, fiscal deficit hawks have become the dominant voices in setting the economic policy agenda. Debates on macroeconomic policy have focused primarily on how much austerity to impose and how quickly, given a perceived overarching imperative of dramatically reducing fiscal deficits. The idea of strengthening the recovery through further stimulus has become a distinctly minority view, at least in mainstream policymaking circles. This is a very dangerous development, reflecting serious misunderstandings about the magnitude of the crisis and the impact of the stimulus program.

Why the deficit hawks are wrong.[1] Deficit hawks in the United States have focused on three major hazards tied to the large-scale federal deficits that have emerged since 2009. They begin with the claim that high levels of government borrowing would drive up interest rates since government borrowing increases the economy's overall demand for credit dramatically without correspondingly increasing the national savings that are the basis for the supply of credit. These high interest rates then produce two more problems: a heavy burden of government debt and strong inflationary pressures.

These issues raised by deficit hawks certainly need to be considered seriously. But how exactly we should act on our concerns should be guided by the facts of the situation. Two facts in particular are crucial as starting points: the interest rates of U.S. government bonds, including long-term bonds, have been at historically low levels since the Obama stimulus program was introduced (as of this writing, we are able to observe data from March 2009–January 2012); and, similarly, the inflation rate has been subdued throughout this full period.

Why have interest rates on government bonds and inflation remained low despite the large deficits? Two factors are at play. The first is that financial market investors globally have been focused on reducing their risks since the financial collapse, in a dramatic reversal of their mindset during the bubble years. Within that mindset, investors have been voting strongly in support of U.S. government bonds as the single safest store of their wealth. The European fiscal crisis that began in the spring of 2010 and has continued into 2012 provides yet another reminder that, however bad conditions are in the United States, they can easily become worse someplace else.

The second factor has been the Federal Reserve's aggressive policies to hold down interest rates. This includes the Fed's near-zero interest rate policy for their target short-term rate, the federal funds rate. In addition, the Fed has also successfully lowered the longer-term rates on U.S. Treasury Bonds under the policy they have termed "quantitative easing." At the same time, as we will discuss below, none of the Fed measures have succeeded in pushing down the long-term rates at which *nonfinancial businesses borrow* to anywhere near the extent that the Fed has pushed down the short-term federal funds rate available to commercial banks or the longer-term U.S. Treasury Bond rates.

As for lack of inflationary pressure, this is a direct result of the high rate of unemployment and low rate of capacity utilization, which imply little upward pressure on wages and prices. As the Harvard economist Martin Feldstein, one of the most prominent deficit hawks, acknowledges, "Sustained budget deficits . . . do not cause inflation unless they lead to excess demand for goods and labor" (2010). The other factor that could create inflationary pressures is an upward jolt in global oil prices, which in turn produces a sharp rise in gasoline prices at the pump. The price of gasoline at the pump did spike during 2011, rising as high as $4 per gallon in May 2011. But even this didn't cause a rise of overall inflation in the United States, demonstrating that any other upward price pressures in the United States economy have been nonexistent.

The reality of low interest rates, in particular, also greatly alleviates concerns about worsening long-term debt burdens. Despite historically large fiscal deficits, the federal government is now paying interest on the total outstanding debt at a rate that is historically low, not high. As such, while it is true that the government will need to reduce its borrowing once the recession is behind us, *there is no short-term crisis* whatsoever in terms of the government's ability to pay off debt obligations it faces now or over the next few years.

Why didn't the stimulus end the recession?[2] If the fiscal expansion did not cause interest rates, inflation, or the government's interest payment burden to rise significantly, why didn't the economy respond more positively to the large-scale injection of fiscal stimulus?

One possible explanation, coming from a major variant of neoliberal orthodoxy called New Classical economics, is straightforward. The Obama stimulus failed because it was never capable of succeeding. This is due to what the Harvard University economist Robert Barro calls "Ricardian equivalence," the argument that households and businesses view government deficits as creating increased future tax liabilities for themselves. As such, they anticipate these future tax burdens in their present behavior by reducing present levels of spending, more or less by the amount that their future tax burden will rise. The rise in deficit-financed government spending will therefore be matched by an equivalent reduction in private-sector spending— that is, the stimulus effects of a government deficit–financed anti-recession program will be zero.

However, Barro's notion of Ricardian equivalence has always rested on an implausible set of behavioral assumptions, including that businesses and households operate with perfect foresight within the context of perfectly functioning financial markets. This is how they are able to calculate accurately their future tax burdens associated with current fiscal deficits. In fact, there is no way anybody could know all the things that Barro blithely asserts everyone knows as a matter of course. His model also assumes that households and businesses will always choose to save more money now to cover these future tax burdens rather than, at least in some substantial number of cases, spend more now and worry about the future later.

Other economists have argued on empirical grounds that the Obama stimulus policies did not produce its intended results. Probably the most prominent representative of this view is John Taylor, a Stanford economist and former high official in the George W. Bush Treasury Department. Taylor claims that his empirical findings support the Barro-type position on why the stimulus program was bound to fail. However a careful reading of Taylor's findings tells a different story: that the stimulus failed because of the specific ways in which it was implemented, not—as with Barro—because it was doomed to failure no matter what.

According to the evidence presented by Taylor, the problem with the stimulus was that that too much government support went either to tax cuts or to support state and local governments experiencing severe budgetary crises.

Taylor correctly identifies several problems with channeling stimulus funds in these ways. First, households and businesses that received tax cuts used most of the extra money either to pay off old debts or to increase savings. They did not increase their spending by a significant amount. In addition, support for state and local governments was simply inadequate. During the recession, tax revenues fell precipitously because of the corresponding falls in incomes, spending, and property values. At the same time, the recession meant that people's needs for state services such as Medicaid and home heating assistance rose sharply. The result was that the stimulus funds provided for state and local governments covered only about one-third of their overall budget shortfalls in 2009 and 2010. Most of the rest of the gap was covered through state and local governments enacting budget cuts. This meant that, on balance, state and local governments were reducing their spending overall, even after taking account of their federal stimulus support.

Overall, both the support for households and businesses through tax cuts and the support the stimulus provided for state and local governments did help prevent the economy's floor from collapsing altogether. But the severity of the recession was such that these measures could do little, if anything, to inject new spending into the economy. We can see this more clearly by considering the two larger obstacles—indeed major headwinds—that weakened the effects of the Obama stimulus still further. These were the collapse of household wealth and the breakdown of credit flowing for productive investments and job creation, especially for small businesses.

Evaporation of household wealth. Figure 2 shows the movements of real household wealth in the United States between 2001 and September 2011. As the figure makes clear, household wealth rose sharply between 2002 and 2006, from $51.0 trillion to $70.7 trillion, in step with the inflating financial bubble. But household wealth then collapsed along with the bubble—falling by $17.6 trillion from 2006 to 2008, to $53.1 trillion, a nearly 25 percent decline in just two years. Even with household wealth having recovered somewhat by the end of 2011, it was still, at $58.4 trillion, 17.4 percent below the 2006 peak.

Research examining the impact of changes in household wealth on consumption generally finds that households will reduce their spending by between three to five cents for every dollar of wealth that they lose, i.e., a wealth effect of between 3–5 percent in total spending relative to the change in household wealth.[3] Thus, even taking the lower-end 3 percent estimate, the loss of $17.6 trillion in household wealth would imply a roughly $525 billion reduction in household spending. This figure is two-thirds the total amount of the two-year stimulus package of $787 billion.

Figure 2. U.S. Household Net Worth, 2001 - 2011
In Trillions
(inflation-adjusted 2011 dollars)

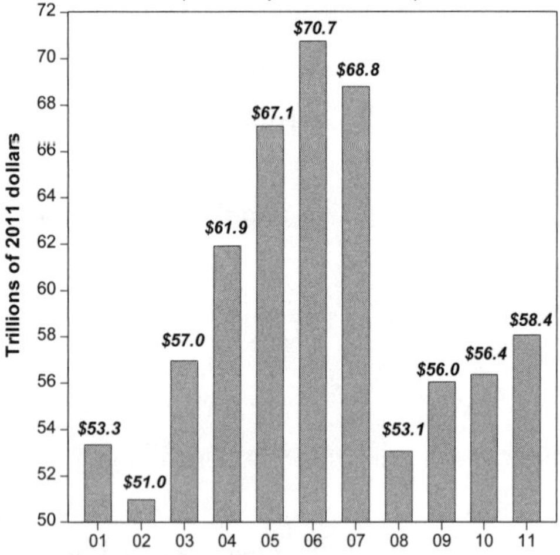

Source: Balance Sheets of U.S. Economy
Note: Inflation adjustment with CPI-U.

Credit market lockout for smaller businesses. Figure 3 shows the dramatic contraction in business borrowing and lending resulting from the 2008–09 financial crisis and recession. As we see, borrowing by non-financial corporations fell from $871 billion to $4.3 billion between 2007 and 2009. Corporate borrowing did then recover fairly strongly in 2010–11. However, the pattern is much more severe for non-corporate businesses, including most smaller businesses. Among these firms, borrowing fell from $526 billion in 2007 to negative $346 billion in 2009. This was a $900 billion reversal of financial flows, equal to roughly 6 percent of GDP. Money that had been coming into smaller businesses for new investments and job creation flowed out in debt repayments. This pattern continued through 2011, with non-corporate firms still undertaking virtually no net borrowing, three years after the Wall Street bust.

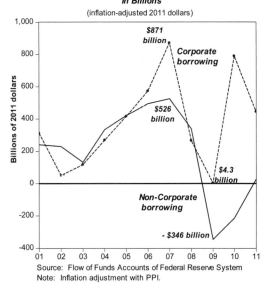

Figure 3. U.S. Nonfinancial Corporate and Non-Corporate Business Borrowing, 2001 - 2011
In Billions

(inflation-adjusted 2011 dollars)

Source: Flow of Funds Accounts of Federal Reserve System
Note: Inflation adjustment with PPI.

This severe decline in net borrowing and lending for smaller, non-corporate businesses, reflects an on-going attitude of hunkering down and avoiding new risk on the parts of both borrowers and lenders. Of course, businesses are reluctant to borrow and invest when they observe weak conditions in their target markets. That is precisely why austerity measures, such as those that have been enacted at the state and local government levels, are only worsening prospects for a healthy recovery.

At the same time, a weak market is not the only factor holding back the flow of credit to smaller businesses. In fact, there is strong evidence that a high proportion of small businesses have been willing to borrow to expand their operations in spite of the poor recovery, but that they have been denied credit at a price they can afford. A summer 2011 survey by Pepperdine University's Graziadio School of Business and Management found that, at that time, 95 percent of business owners reported wanting to execute a growth strategy, but only 53 percent were obtaining the funding they needed to execute their strategy. At the same time, bankers were reporting that they were rejecting 60 percent of their loan applications. An October 2010 survey by the Federal Reserve Bank of New York found similar results. The Fed survey found that roughly three-quarters of those who applied for credit were either turned down outright or had only part of their request met, with fully one-third receiving no funds.

In addition to businesses getting their loan applications turned down outright, borrowing rates for average businesses have remained relatively high through the recession, even while, thanks to Federal Reserve policy, commercial banks have been able to borrow at near-zero rates since the beginning of 2009. We can see this in Figure 4, which shows the monthly movements of the Federal Reserve's target policy rate, the federal funds rate, and the Baa corporate borrowing rate from 2001 through December 2011. The Baa rate applies to corporations that are safe enough to obtain an investment-grade bond rating while still being at the high-risk end of investment-grade firms. The rates that would apply to non-corporate businesses would generally be higher than the Baa rate, as they would be perceived as being more risky than an average corporation. As Figure 4 shows, the Baa rate has fallen since 2009, but the decline has been modest, especially given the Fed's extremely accommodating policy stance. That is, the Baa rate as of December 2011 was 5.3 percent, only modestly lower than the

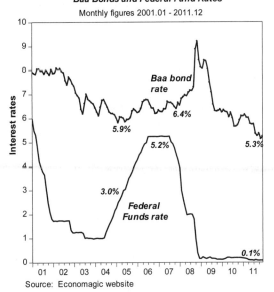

Figure 4. Interest Rates for Business Borrowers vs Commercial Banks

Baa Bonds and Federal Fund Rates

Monthly figures 2001.01 - 2011.12

Source: Economagic website

Baa rate of 5.9 percent when the federal funds rate was at 3.0 percent. Even when the Fed was holding the federal funds rate as high as 5.2 percent, the Baa rate was only averaging about 6.4 percent.

Cash and liquid asset hoarding by banks and corporations.[4] An even more dramatic indicator of the ongoing malfunctioning of the U.S. financial system is that, as of this writing in January 2012, U.S. commercial banks and large corporations are sitting on huge hoards of cash and other liquid assets. Specifically, as of January 2012, the commercial banks were carrying an unprecedented $1.6 trillion in cash reserves. They obtained most of this money through the Federal Reserve having maintained the interest rate at which banks can borrow at nearly zero percent—that is, the banks have access to nearly unlimited liquid funds at no borrowing costs. In addition, U.S. nonfinancial corporations were holding about $2 trillion in liquid assets. They are using a large proportion of these funds to engage in financial engineering, such as buying back shares of their own stocks, as opposed to investing in new productive equipment and expanding their operations. The total of cash with the banks and liquid assets held by big corporations thus amounts to $3.6 trillion, equal to about 23 percent of U.S. GDP.

Of course, I recognize that a significant fraction of these funds needs to be held by banks and corporations to carry an adequate margin of safety in the currently highly risky environment. However, in research that my co-authors and I published in December 2011, we assessed how much of that total $3.6 trillion was needed as a safety margin of cash and liquid assets and how much could be considered as hoards of excessive liquid asset holdings. After making highly conservative assumptions about the safety requirements of the banks and non-financial corporations in the environment of 2011–12, we concluded that the *excess* liquid holdings of the private sector were about $1.4 trillion, with $1 trillion held by the commercial banks and the remaining $400 billion by the nonfinancial corporations.

ROBERT POLLIN   87

One crucial question to ask with respect to these outsized liquid asset hoards is: what would employment be in the U.S. if some significant share of these funds were channeled into the expansion of productive activities and investments by private businesses? My co-authors and I found that U.S. employment could expand by about *19 million jobs*—from roughly 140 to 159 million people being employed in the U.S.—in 2012–14 if only $1.4 trillion of the total $3.6 trillion are used for productive business investments and job creation. An increase of 19 million jobs in the U.S. economy over 2012–14 would then drive the official unemployment rate down from its level over 2011 of around 9 percent to below 5 percent by the end of 2014.

A Short-term Agenda for Job Creation

Private businesses operate to earn a profit. As such, the fact that banks and non-financial corporations are sitting on approximately $1.4 trillion in excess liquidity rather than expanding their businesses and hiring workers must mean that, at some level, they do not see adequate profit opportunities in the U.S. economy today through investments and job creation.

We therefore need to explore a range of policy approaches that can expand overall demand in the economy, reduce the level of risk for borrowers and lenders, and/or raise the costs for banks and non-financial corporations to continue holding excess liquid assets. These policy approaches include further federal stimulus initiatives, measures to reduce the existing debt burdens of homeowners, taxing the excess reserves of banks, and extending federal loan guarantees for small businesses.

Before delving into details on various short-run recovery measures, we do need to ask: is this really still necessary? As of early 2012, two-and-a-half years after the recession had officially been declared over, evidence was finally mounting that unemployment is falling steadily. The official unemployment rate for January 2012 was 8.3 percent, a substantial improvement relative to January 2010, at 9.7 percent, and January

2011, at 9.1 percent. But let's assume that with these recent improved employment figures, this recovery will end up proceeding at more or less the normal rate of progress relative to recent recessions. Yet even under such a "normal" scenario, unemployment would not likely fall to around 5 percent under early 2017. We would not likely hit four percent unemployment until mid-2018, assuming the recovery could be kept going for another six years.[5] As such, even amid the 2012 recovery, assuming it holds, there remains a pressing need to greatly accelerate the rate of job creation.

Continued federal government stimulus spending. Given inadequate demand in the economy, it is imperative for the federal government to proceed through a new round of fiscal stimulus policies until the recession is clearly behind us. Expanding government spending is the only way to establish a solid floor to overall market demand. Business can then begin evaluating opportunities to invest and expand, with a basic level of assurance that the markets they are targeting will not collapse in the near future.

Many features of the jobs program proposed by President Obama in September 2011 can serve effectively in this regard, as long as the levels of government spending are sufficiently large. The most important targets for new spending proposed by Obama include new rounds of support for state and local governments, extending unemployment insurance benefits, and recommitting government funds for public investments in infrastructure, education and the green economy. The amounts devoted to these areas should be at least as large as the roughly $400 billion per year that was budgeted through the ARRA. A new fiscal stimulus of sufficiently large magnitude should then help encourage commercial banks and nonfinancial corporations to see growing profit opportunities, and thus to begin moving a significant share of their cash hoards into productive investments.

Monetary and credit market policies. Monetary policy has certainly been expansionary by any conventional measure since the recession began. This is evident from the Federal Reserve's policy interest rate, the federal funds rate, being held at near zero since the recession began. However, the real aim of expansionary monetary policy must be to produce conditions in credit markets that will encourage household spending and business investments, which in turn can generate millions of decent jobs. Indeed, the more apt term here should be "credit market policy" as opposed to "monetary policy." It is therefore crucial now that the Federal Reserve and federal government work in common to advance direct credit market policies that compliment federal stimulus spending to stabilize and raise the overall level of demand in the economy. There is a range of live options to pursue along these lines.

Debt forgiveness. One important set of approaches is focused around banks writing off a significant share of their outstanding household debts, starting with the mortgage debts of the 10.9 million homeowners who remain underwater with their mortgagers. That amounts to 22.5 percent of all residential properties with mortgages. There is a twofold logic to such proposals. The first is that, since the crisis began in 2008, the banks have been given extraordinary levels of support to keep them functioning, even while giving out outsized bonuses to their top executives. The bailout operations at the outset of the crisis are the most obvious examples. But as we have discussed above, maintaining the Federal Reserve's policy interest rate at near zero for two and a half years has been the basis for enabling the banks to build up $1.6 trillion in cash reserves, as of the most recent data. With cash reserves at this extraordinary level, the banks are currently well fortified to write off all of their nonperforming mortgage loans and still have more than $1 trillion available to support new lending.

From the other side, if homeowners generally, and those that are underwater with their mortgages most immediately, could receive some significant debt relief, this would enable them to start spending again. This shift in the households' budgetary situation would thus provide a boost to overall market demand.

Taxing excess bank reserves and guaranteeing small business loans. Another approach would combine two initiatives, one carrot and one stick. The carrot would be measures to substantially reduce the level of risk being faced by both borrowers and lenders. This can be done through the government's existing loan guarantee program. In 2009, the total level of loans guaranteed by the Federal government was about $340 billion. The two largest categories were subsidized mortgage and student loans. About $50 billion went to business loans, through the Small Business Administration and Export-Import Bank. In the current climate, the federal government could consider roughly doubling its overall loan guarantee program—that is, inject another $300 billion in guaranteed loans into the credit market, and shift the focus of the new guarantee programs to business. Overall guarantees would therefore be about $600 billion, with a $300 billion increase from 2009. For this initiative to be effective at reducing risk and encouraging new investment, the terms on the guaranteed loans will have to be generous—that is very large guarantees, in the range of 90 percent; low or no fees on the loans; and low interest rates for borrowers.

The stick would be for the federal government to tax the excess reserves now held by banks. This should create a strong disincentive for banks to continue holding massive cash hoards. It is difficult to know in advance what the appropriate tax rate should be for this purpose—probably in the range of 1–2 percent. But any such initiative should also allow government to operate with flexibility, to adjust the rate as needed for channeling excess reserves into job-generating investments. This could be implemented by the Federal Reserve acting on its own, by setting a "maximum reserve" level that would be comparable to the existing minimum reserve requirements the banks now face. If a bank exceeded the maximum reserve level, they would then have to pay a fee to the Fed. The Fed could take the first small step along these lines by ending their current policy of actually paying banks 0.25 percent interest on their reserve holdings, which only encourages hoarding. The reason the Fed gives for paying interest to banks to hoard cash is that it discourages banks from lending too much money quickly to consumers and businesses. This, according to the Fed's reasoning, could encourage inflation, once the consumers and businesses start spending their new supply of borrowed funds. But shouldn't it be obvious by now that the overriding problem in the economy today is not excessive inflation, but grossly inadequate job opportunities?

One crucial feature of this combination of policies is that its impact on the federal budget will be negligible. Loan guarantees are contingent liabilities for the federal government. This means that, beyond some relatively modest increase in administrative costs, the government would incur costs from the loan guarantee program only as a result of defaults on the guaranteed loans. Even if we assumed, implausibly, that the default rate on the new loans was triple the proportion that prevailed in 2007, prior to the recession, this would still increase the federal budget by less than 1 percent. Moreover, a significant share of this budgetary expense could be covered by the revenues generated by the excess reserve tax. Overall, then, this combination of policies provides a low-cost route for pushing the economy to where it needs to be—that is, on the path toward full employment.

5

*Building a Sustainable
Full Employment Economy*

How do we create a sustainable full employment economy over the long run? I focus here on four crucial areas:

1) Dramatically increasing investments in the areas of clean energy and education, and correspondingly reducing spending on conventional energy sources—including fossil fuels and nuclear power—and the military. This shift in investment priorities will generate a major expansion of job opportunities at all levels of the economy. These major employment benefits will be in addition to the intrinsic benefits of controlling climate change and increasing educational opportunities.

2) Industrial policies to undergird the clean energy transformation and, more broadly, to promote a revived, innovative U.S. manufacturing sector.

3) Financial regulatory policies that direct the financial system toward promoting productive investments, the green economy, job creation, and financial stability, and away from the hyper-speculative practices that increasingly dominated our economic trajectory over a generation.

4) Fiscal policies that can maintain the long-term federal government deficit within a reasonable range without imposing austerity, while also supporting a return to a more egalitarian society.

Clean Energy and Education for Job Creation

We can begin to envision the path to creating a sustainable full employment economy through considering some basic data on the relative job-creating effects of spending within different sectors of the U.S. economy.[1] The data reported in Figure 5 show the level of job creation in each of four sectors—clean energy, education, fossil fuels and the military—for every $1 million in spending in these sectors. By a significant margin, education is the most effective source of job creation among these alternatives—about 27 jobs per $1 million in spending. Clean energy investments are second, with about 17 jobs per $1 million of spending. The U.S. military creates about 11.2 jobs, while spending within the fossil fuel sector, by far the weakest source of job creation per dollars, creates about 5 jobs per $1 million.

Figure 5. Job Creation in the U.S. through $1 Million in Spending

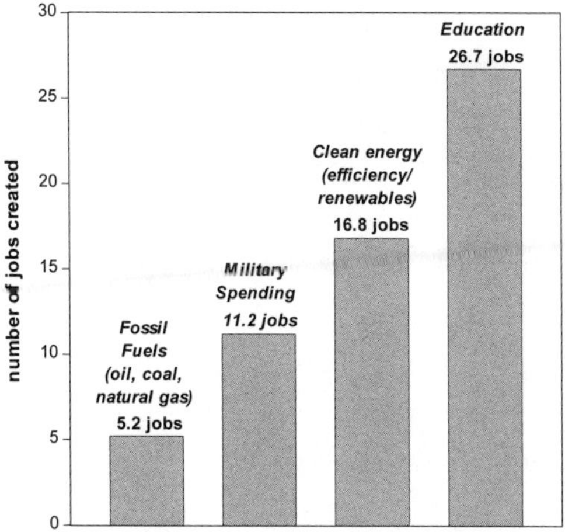

Sources: Pollin, Heintz, and Garrett-Peltier (2009); Pollin and Garrett-Peltier (2011)

These figures combine three categories of job creation—what are termed *direct, indirect,* and *induced* job creation—that result through spending on any activity. Direct jobs are those created by an activity itself, such as building a wind turbine, hiring school teachers, opening a military base in Afghanistan, or transporting oil from the Persian Gulf to Houston. Indirect jobs are those generated by businesses providing supplies to support the direct activities, such as steel manufacturers supplying a wind turbine manufacturer, or a paper company providing office supplies to a school, military base, or an oil company's corporate headquarters. The term "induced jobs" refers to the expansion of employment that results when people who are newly hired—either through direct or indirect job creation—spend the money they have begun to earn. This is also frequently termed the "multiplier effect" of direct and indirect job creation. These multiplier effects that generate induced jobs are especially beneficial in offering expanding market opportunities for small businesses, such as food service firms selling lunches at a wind-energy work site.

Two main factors account for the differences in total job creation across sectors, including all direct, indirect, and induced jobs. The first is *relative labor intensity*, the amount of people, as opposed to everything else, a business utilizes in its operations. For example, a clean energy investment program utilizes far more of its budget to hire people than to acquire machines, supplies, land (either on- or offshore), or energy itself.

The second factor is relative domestic content per overall spending amount—how much of the work is done within the United States rather than other countries. The clean energy sector relies much more than the fossil fuel sector on economic activities taking place within the United States—such as retrofitting homes or upgrading the electrical grid system—and less on imports.

In addition, while average wages in both education and clean energy are about 10–20 percent lower than those in the military and fossil fuel sectors, the absolute numbers of jobs created in education and clean energy are so much higher that these investments produce far more high-paying as well as low-paying jobs than spending on either the military or fossil fuels.

Consider an agenda in which we transfer about 25 percent of total spending in both the military ($690 billion) and fossil fuel ($635 billion) sectors—about $330 billion per year—in equal shares into education and clean energy. Before assessing the effect of this transfer of spending priorities on employment, we should of course also recognize their crucial and complimentary political and environmental benefits. Reducing the Pentagon's budget by 25 percent would simply return the military to its spending level prior to the wars in Iraq and Afghanistan, which is fully consistent with the Obama administration having already ended major spending on Iraq and pledging to end the Afghanistan war by the end of 2012.

Cutting spending from fossil fuels and transferring it into clean energy of course reflects the imperative of controlling CO_2 emissions to fight global climate change. Indeed, if we are going to meet widely recognized minimum level of reductions to stabilize average global temperatures at acceptable levels—80 percent below our 2000 level as of 2050—we will need to reduce fossil fuel spending by far more over the coming generation. Finally, transferring approximately $165 billion per year into spending on education would represent a roughly 16 percent increase over the current total public spending level of about $1 trillion. An increase in educational funding of this magnitude could mean, for example, reducing average classroom sizes nationwide from 23 to 19 students per class, plus an increase of $1,500 in the average amount of financial aid for college students, plus substantial improvements in school buildings throughout the country—or some appropriate combination of these and other priorities.

In terms of employment effects, the impact of a $330 billion annual spending shift out of the military and fossil fuel sectors and into education and clean energy would be dramatic. It would create about 4.8 million more jobs for a given level of total spending. The job expansion would be across all sectors and activities—i.e., new opportunities for highly paid engineers, researchers, lawyers and business consultants as well as for elementary school teachers, carpenters, bus drivers, cleaning staff at hotels, and lunch-counter workers at wind energy construction sites.

In the context of today's economy, the injection of 4.8 million new jobs in short order would also reduce the unemployment rate by about one-third, from about 9 to 6 percent. However, this kind of large-scale shift in spending economy-wide will not occur rapidly enough to affect today's unemployment rate, in contrast with the policy measures presented in Chapter 4. But this large-scale shift in the country's investment priorities is capable of transforming the employment picture over the long-term. For example, assume that the unemployment rate could fall over the next two years, if only to, say, 7 percent, through some combination of government interventions from the Obama administration and Federal Reserve along with something akin to a normal pattern of recovery. Within such a scenario, 4.8 million additional jobs through a spending shift would drop the 7 percent unemployment rate to 3.9 percent. At this point, we would be at an unemployment rate where, in both the 1960s and 1990s, workers also saw major gains in bargaining power and rising real wages. Poverty also fell significantly in both periods when unemployment fell below 4 percent. In short, this kind of shift in investment priorities—toward clean energy and education and away from fossil fuels and the military—can be the foundation for building a sustainable full employment economy.

The Need for Industrial Policies[2]

To proceed successfully with a clean energy/education investment agenda will of course entail a range of strong and effective public policy interventions. It is fair to question whether the United States government possesses the capacity to mount such industrial-based policies over the long term. My own short answer to this question is an emphatic "yes." I say this while fully recognizing the widely held view that the United States has no record of success, or even of serious effort, at undertaking industrial policies.

In reality the United States already practices industrial policy, and has done so for a long time. But the problem is that industrial policy in the United States operates primarily through the Pentagon. This has produced dramatically varying results. On the one hand, military-based industrial policy has supported epoch-defining technical breakthroughs, including jet aviation, the computer, and the Internet. It has also produced a steady stream of pork-barrel opportunities and scandals. But industrial policies in the United States also extend beyond the Pentagon, frequently operating without a clear sense of purpose, sometimes even at cross-purposes.

More precisely, then, the United States today operates with a variety of industrial policies—in fact, too many. If we are going to successfully proceed with a unified agenda for full employment and the green economy, what we really need are industrial policy measures that are more carefully designed, focused, and executed. This will entail building from the major successes that have been achieved, as well as gaining greater understanding of and power over the forces that produce failures.

What is industrial policy? Although there are other ways the term can be used, industrial policy is often associated closely with the concept of a "developmental state." As one key element within a developmental state, industrial policy generally focuses on promoting research and development (R&D), moving the technical innovations emerging from R&D investments into commercial use, and raising productivity and competiveness by getting businesses to adopt these innovations as rapidly as possible.

But we need to clarify this broad idea further. This is because, with industrial policy as a tool of a developmental state, a range of policy instruments and targets can be put into play. These could include

R&D subsidies for government, university, or private-business research centers. It could also include preferential tax treatment, credit opportunities, or direct subsidies for specific sectors of the economy, different regions, or even individual business firms. Some types of business regulations—such as auto fuel-efficiency standards, or financial regulations aimed at channeling credit to preferred sectors, or activities at subsidized rates—could also be seen as industrial policy interventions.

How industrial policy operates in the United States. An important feature of much of the U.S. experience with industrial policies has been that these policies have been frequently implemented for purposes other than to promote technology, productivity, competitiveness, and jobs. Since World War II, motivations behind the use of industrial policies have included:

1. Bailing out the U.S. auto industry. In 2008 and 2009, General Motors (GM) and Chrysler received $65 billion in loans from the federal government. The loans were provided both by the then-outgoing

Bush administration in December 2008, as well as the newly installed Obama administration in March 2009. This action was taken after both automakers had testified before Congress that, without major federal assistance, they would be forced into bankruptcy. These bailouts had an important precedent in the 1979 government bailout of Chrysler. In this prior case, the federal government provided $1.5 billion worth of loan guarantees (equivalent to about $3.5 billion in 2009 dollars), as well as "voluntary" quotas on foreign cars being imported into U.S. markets.

One can make a reasonable case for both bailouts on the grounds that, in 1979 as well as in 2009, the collapse of GM and Chrysler would have caused massive unemployment and more general economic hardship, especially in the Midwest. But when the tools of industrial policy are cobbled together amid a crisis, we cannot expect the results to be stellar, beyond preventing the firms from shutting down outright. The 2009 GM bailout, for example, imposed devastating concessions on autoworkers, including the elimination of 21,000 union jobs, while the United Auto Workers itself had to accept GM stock of uncertain value to replace $10 billion in guaranteed health care funds.

2. States and municipalities competing to attract businesses. Over the past four decades, states and municipalities in the U.S. have competed among themselves, sometimes intensively, to attract businesses to locate with them. The main weapon in this competition has been various types of tax incentives. Foreign auto companies have been among the most favored recipients of such support, including, just since 2006: Kia Motors receiving a reported $400 million from West Point, Georgia; Honda receiving $141 million from Greensburg, Indiana; Toyota getting $300 million from Blue Springs, Mississippi; and Volkswagen obtaining $577 million from Chattanooga, Tennessee. These efforts have achieved some success in their primary aim of attracting businesses to their location. But they have done so almost entirely on a zero-sum basis—that is, by reducing job

creation in neighboring states and localities that have not offered the same incentives.

3. National defense. Unlike with the auto industry bailouts and state-level tax-break competitions, national defense-related industrial policies have produced spectacular successes. Commercial-level use of jet aviation, computers, and the Internet—all transformational technologies that define the U.S. and all other modern economies—were products of industrial policies directed and financed by the Pentagon.

Do U.S. industrial policies have to run through the pentagon to succeed? The key factor of Pentagon-centered industrial policy is the combination—on a massive scale and over a sustained time period—of R&D investment spending, plus the maintaining of a guaranteed market through procurements. This idea is the main theme in the important recent book by Vernon Ruttan, *Is War Necessary for Economic Growth? Military Procurement and Technology Development* (2006). Ruttan emphasizes that R&D alone would not have brought new technologies to the point of commercial success. It was also necessary that, over the course of decades, the military provided a guaranteed market for new technologies. This enabled the technologies to incubate over time without having to prematurely face the test of the market.

In principle, this combination could be replicated under some auspices other than the Pentagon. An obvious priority here would be to build manufacturing capacity around clean energy technologies, including green buses and rail cars, as well as automobiles. Investments in these areas could be the basis for a revival of a transformed U.S. auto industry.

Similar programs could be advanced for public investments in renewable energy projects, such as developing the offshore wind energy potential of the Great Lakes region. The major question is whether the government can justify the combination of large-scale R&D spending and procurement that would be necessary for such initiatives to succeed. The only basis on which this can occur is in terms of some standard of broadly shared social welfare. The issue of developing an effective set of industrial policies around an agenda of clean energy, transportation, and manufacturing at this point becomes political. For example, can a strong enough political movement be mounted to mobilize the government's capacities to build widely accessible public transportation systems and large-scale wind farms in a manner similar to what it has already accomplished so spectacularly through the Pentagon?

Not surprisingly, reaching that level of political influence poses numerous challenges of its own. To begin with, few people outside of elite policy-making circles in the U.S. appreciate the extent to which the federal government has been successful in conducting industrial policies. Instead, as Fred Block (2008) argues, U.S. industrial policies have operated as what he terms a "hidden developmental state," under the umbrella of the Pentagon's national security agenda, not as an open public policy effort to advance technical innovation, productivity, competitiveness, and jobs.

Conducting industrial policies in the U.S. in this way has meant that the military has exercised disproportionate influence over what passes as legitimate aims of such policies. And precisely because Pentagon-based industrial policies have been sheltered from the normal standards of public review, an adequate system of carrots and sticks has never emerged to regulate the private businesses that benefit most directly from these policies through contracts and subsidies. The egregious non-competitive, gold-plated, cost-plus contracts handed out to weapons suppliers are the most well known examples of this broader problem.

Here, then, is the overarching challenge in trying to design industrial policies to advance clean energy, a reconfigured transportation system, and a renewed manufacturing sector. As a technical matter, the federal government has the capacity today to dramatically expand the markets for clean public transportation and renewable energy systems, just as the Pentagon spent forty years nurturing the Internet. But we lack the experience and political will to advance this agenda outside of the defense establishment. The challenge then is to figure out ways to strengthen such capacities as quickly as possible.

Financial Regulation for Ending Wall Street Dominance[3]

Full employment cannot be sustained as long as Wall Street is free to operate the financial system as if it were a casino. Establishing a new system of effective financial regulations is therefore an imperative.

President Obama signed into law the Dodd-Frank Wall Street Reform and Consumer Protection Act in July 2010. Dodd-Frank is the most ambitious measure aimed at regulating U.S. financial markets since the Glass-Steagall Act was implemented in the midst of the 1930s Depression. However, it remains an open question as to whether Dodd-Frank is capable of controlling the hyper-speculative practices that produced the near total global financial collapse of 2008–09, which in turn brought the mass unemployment that we experienced through 2011 and into 2012.

Dodd-Frank is a massive piece of legislation, 875 pages in length, covering a wide range of issues. These include coordinating the efforts of the Federal Reserve, Treasury, Securities and Exchange Commission, (SEC) and other financial regulatory agencies to control excessive speculation; creating the Consumer Financial Protection Bureau; establishing regulatory controls on the previously unregulated hedge funds and derivative markets; and restricting the ability of big banks, such as Goldman Sachs, to trade on their own corporate accounts when they are supposed to be focused on their clients' interests only, a practice known as "proprietary trading."

The prevailing view among progressive commentators is that Dodd-Frank was a major victory for Wall Street. There are valid reasons to reach that conclusion. The most important is, despite its length, Dodd-Frank mostly lays out a broad regulatory framework, allowing the various regulatory agencies to settle on the details of implementation over the next few years. Both Wall Street lobbyists as well as advocates for strong regulation anticipate that the lobbyists will be able to dominate this process of detailed rulemaking. But the reality is more complex. In fact, Dodd-Frank remains contested terrain because there are lots of areas where strong regulations can emerge through this detailed rulemaking process.

Terms of engagement. The very fact that Dodd-Frank exists demonstrates that the glory days for financial deregulators are mercifully over for the foreseeable future. Yet Wall Street is clearly moving into the phase of regulatory rulemaking with a strong hand. The major Wall Street firms have huge budgets at their disposal to intervene at will during the process of detailed rule-setting. In addition, the regulators themselves understand that they can burnish their future private sector career prospects if they are solicitous to the concerns of Wall Street while still working for Uncle Sam.

These are unavoidable realities. But the ammunition on behalf of serious reform is also powerful. It begins with the overwhelming evidence provided by the financial meltdown itself that weakly regulated financial markets produce economic disasters. The final version of Dodd-Frank that was passed into law testifies to this. Despite the ambiguities included in the final law, many features of the measure were actually strengthened through the drafting process, as lobbying efforts by Americans for Financial Reform and other citizens' groups did end up exerting influence over many important issues. An important example is the regulations that were established around derivative markets, including the markets for options and futures contracts, swap agreements and other complex financial instruments. The version of the bill that passed in the Senate was much tougher than the House version in requiring, for example, derivatives to be traded on regulated exchanges, as opposed to being permitted to operate in unregulated, freewheeling over-the-counter markets. Wall Street was quite displeased when, despite their intensive lobbying efforts, the final version of Dodd-Frank that emerged out of the reconciliation conference between the House and Senate members ended up much closer to what the Senate had drafted.

There is another important consideration here. In fact, it is not necessary for the supporters of effective regulations to win victories on each and every rule that needs to be hammered out. Rather, reformers can achieve a great deal winning victories in a few key areas within the full expanse of Dodd-Frank. We can see this by considering one crucial case in point, the features of Dodd-Frank covering proprietary trading by the giant banks.

Taming the banks' proprietary trading through the Volcker Rule. The Volcker Rule is not actually one rule, but a series of measures, which were strongly supported by former Federal Reserve Chair Paul Volcker. Their purpose is to greatly limit propriety trading and related highly risky and destabilizing activities by Goldman Sachs, J.P. Morgan, Citibank and other mega-banks. The precise ways in which these rules will be implemented are still being hotly debated as of this writing in January 2012. Predictably, Republicans in Congress and the regulatory agencies, working along with lobbyists for the banking industry, have been working assiduously to both delay implementation of any version of the Volcker Rule and to ensure that the version that is ultimately implemented is heavily watered down.

Propriety trading and related activities by the big banks were a major cause of the financial bubble as well as the collapse of the bubble and near total global meltdown in 2008–09. The banks ran large trading books—inventories of securities that they themselves own—ostensibly so that this supply of securities would be readily available for their clients to purchase. But maintaining large trading books enabled the banks to operate with inside information on their clients' trading patterns. This allowed the banks to stay ahead of market movements, which could be quite profitable for them, sometimes even at the expense of their own clients. For example, J.P. Morgan traders could see which securities their clients wanted to buy. The Morgan traders could then buy those securities first, before prices rose as a result of their clients' increased demand. The Morgan traders would then have the option to sell these securities as soon as the prices rose, again staying crucial steps ahead of their clients in cashing out at a profit.

In addition, the banks' proprietary trading activities were closely intertwined with hedge funds and private equity funds, which, unlike the banks themselves, were essentially unregulated. This allowed the banks to finance proprietary trades with huge pools of unregulated money, raising the risk exposure to all parties involved. It was precisely interconnections such as these that fueled the credit market bubble and subsequent crash.

Dodd-Frank includes measures that could prove effective in dramatically reducing the risks associated with the banks' proprietary trading. First, the legislation includes a blanket prohibition against banks engaging in transactions involving material conflicts of interest or highly risky trading activities. For example, the J.P. Morgan proprietary trading practice I described above would now be prohibited by Dodd-Frank.

Dodd-Frank also obliges regulators to impose capital requirements or other quantitative limits on trading, such as margin requirements, on banks. Capital requirements entail that traders maintain a minimal investment of their cash relative to their overall asset holdings, including their stocks, bonds, buildings, land, and machinery. Margin requirements establish that traders use their own cash holdings, in addition to borrowed funds, to make new asset purchases. There are two interrelated purposes to both capital and margin requirements. The first is to discourage excessive trading by limiting the capacity of traders to finance their trades almost entirely with borrowed funds. The second is to force the banks to put a significant amount of their own money at risk— "putting skin in the game," as they say on Wall Street.

At the same time—and here is where we run into trouble with Dodd-Frank—the law allows for exemptions from regulations as well as various ambiguities that could be readily exploited by the banks. Thus, economics Nobel Laureate Joseph Stiglitz laments that "unfortunately, a key part of the legislative strategy of the banks was to get exemptions so that the force of any regulation passed would be greatly attenuated. The result is a Swiss cheese bill—seemingly strong but with large holes" (2010, p. 335). For example, Dodd-Frank permits some proprietary trading as long as such activities support "market-making activities" and "risk-mitigating hedging activities." Down in the bowels of the regulatory agencies, clever Wall Street lawyers could potentially earn lavish fees parsing such details of language with regulators.

Dodd-Frank does indeed include lots of holes. They can and will be filled. The question is, who will do the filling? I am not so naïve as to assume that regulatory standards such as the Volcker rule will be enforced effectively simply because they are written down on paper. But the fact that they are written down on paper does offer real opportunities for serious political engagement and positive outcomes. As such, Dodd-Frank can be used as a framework for building effective regulations. Capturing these opportunities will require combining two things that do not often mesh well—insightful economic analysis and effective political mobilizations. It will be a difficult, but by no means insurmountable, challenge.

A Progressive Agenda for Deficit Control[4]

Let's begin with a simple but crucial point. That is, if the economy can manage to enter into a sustained recovery rather than being pushed into a double-dip recession, the growing economy will itself generate major reductions in the deficit. This is because when unemployment rises in a double-dip recession, the government is faced with huge extra spending burdens through unemployment insurance, food stamps, Medicaid, and related social safety net commitments. Conversely, when people are newly employed, they can support themselves and pay more taxes. For example, the well-known economists Olivier Blanchard and Roberto Perotti (2002; Blanchard is currently chief economist at the International Monetary Fund) found that for the U.S. economy, a one percent increase in GDP will produce a combined improvement in the government's fiscal situation of about 2.1 percent, including both increases in tax revenues and reductions in government transfer payments. Let's assume for the moment that Blanchard and Perotti's estimates hold up as a recovery is sustained, including to the point where unemployment has fallen significantly. Under such circumstances, it follows that, without any increases in tax rates or cuts in spending programs, the U.S. fiscal deficit could probably be cut by $500–600 billion, if unemployment could be driven down to around 4 percent.

As I have discussed above, reaching a goal of 4–5 percent unemployment is realistic. Still, the economic landscape is too cluttered with landmines to count on the attainment of near-full employment to close the long-term deficit gap by itself. It is therefore useful to consider the deficit forecasts over the next decade developed by the Congressional Budget Office (CBO

2011) as a less optimistic framework for addressing the long-run fiscal situation. The CBO presents a range of estimates, based primarily on different assumptions about the prospects for a sustained recovery over the next few years. The midpoint of these different CBO estimates is that, unless significant changes in both tax policies and government spending programs are forthcoming, the federal deficit will average around 5.3 percent of GDP for the next ten years.

As an initial reaction to this midpoint CBO estimate, a fiscal deficit at 5.3 percent of GDP is obviously a huge decline from the deficits at roughly 10 percent of GDP for 2010 and 2011. But deficits in the range of 5 percent of GDP are still well above the average figure of around 2 percent of GDP over the post World War II era. But are long-term deficits at roughly five percent of GDP necessarily a problem? To answer this, it will be useful to briefly consider some basic distinctions between cyclical and structural deficits, i.e. deficits that emerge through recessions versus those that occur over the course of a full business cycle. It is also helpful to distinguish deficits used to finance the government's ongoing operations versus those devoted to productivity-enhancing capital investments.[5]

If the economy is operating at or near full employment, there is no longer any need to finance current expenditures through deficit spending. Indeed, over the course of a full business cycle—including economic expansions as well as recessions—the government's operating budget should be approximately balanced. Running large structural deficits on operating budgets will likely be regressive, i.e., contributing to generating increased inequality. This is because the government interest payments are funded by tax revenues coming primarily from the middle class households. These payments then get transferred to wealthy bondholders and institutional investors, whether they be in New York, Tokyo, London, or Beijing.

In an approximate full employment economy, the legitimate basis for maintaining a fiscal deficit is to finance long-term projects that will enhance the economy's long-run productivity—such as infrastructure projects or investments to build a clean-energy economy. The appropriate level of deficit spending of this type should roughly correspond to the economy's growth rate of productivity (appropriately defined— i.e. investments than move the economy off of carbon-emitting fossil fuels raise the economy's net rate of production of *goods*). The productivity increases, and corresponding rise of per capita GDP, would then generate the revenue increases to cover the added interest expenses in the government's budget. Based on this principle, we should aim to maintain a structural deficit in the range of 2–3 percent of GDP, as opposed to a roughly 5 percent mid-point figure we derive from the alternative CBO projections.

This level of long-term deficit reduction could be achieved through several alternative combinations. I consider here three options that have been at the center of debate in the United States. These are cuts for the health care industry and the military as well as a tax on financial market transactions. We consider them in turn.

Controlling health care costs. The U.S. government spent about $800 billion in 2010 on Medicare and Medicaid, which amounted to 5.6 percent of GDP. Even in its baseline case, the CBO projects this figure to rise to nearly $1.6 trillion or 6.8 percent of GDP by 2020. As was noted regularly during the recently concluded health care debates, the U.S. spends in total—including private spending as well as on Medicare and Medicaid—about twice as much per capita on health care as other highly developed countries such as Canada, Japan and those in Western Europe. This is while these other countries deliver universal health care coverage, longer life expectancies and generally more healthy populations. The problem with the U.S. health care system is that we spend far beyond other countries for drugs, expensive procedures, and especially insurance and administration. We also devote less attention to prevention.

The Obama health care reform bill, the Patient Protection and Affordable Care Act, which became law in April 2010 aimed at controlling these costs—"bending the health care cost curve downward" was the often-stated goal that time. This law does have several worthy features, including the expansion of Medicare as well as subsidies for private health insurance. But it is a matter of spirited debate whether it will succeed in bending downward the cost curve. The CBO projections are pessimistic. However, the 2010 Medicare Trustees Report offers a much more favorable assessment, concluding that "the financial outlook for the Medicare program is substantially improved as a result of the far-reaching changes in the Patient Protection and Affordable Care Act" (2010 Medicare Trustees Report, p. 8).

The Medicare trustees estimate that, as of 2020, the health care reform bill will generate a savings of about 0.6 percent of GDP—that is, nearly $90 billion a year in today's economy. Projecting further into 2080, the trustees estimate that Obama's reforms will reduce Medicaid costs massively, by more than 40 percent relative to GDP.

This is not the place to adjudicate between the CBO and Medicare Trustee's forecasting models. But these differences do underscore the highly tentative nature of any such projections. The Medicare Trustee findings do also highlight another point—that transforming the U.S. health care system so that it comes more closely in line with the other advanced economies can, almost by itself, bring the federal government's structural deficit close to its historical level of around 2 percent of GDP.

However, let's allow that because of the power of the private health insurance and drug companies, the idea of bringing the U.S. health care system fully in line with other advanced economies is unrealistic. It should nevertheless be reasonable to expect that we could achieve at least half the level of available savings through health care reform measures. These would include the recent Obama measures and any additional initiatives aimed especially at establishing controls on the drug and insurance industries. It is reasonable to expect that such savings could reduce the government's annual structural deficit by about $150 billion.

Cutting the military. The U.S. military budget rose from 3 percent of GDP at the end of the Clinton presidency to 4.3 percent at the end of Bush's two terms. Under the Obama administration's budget for 2011, military spending totaled $712 billion, which is 4.7 percent of projected GDP for that year. If the U.S. returned to the 2000 level of military spending relative to GDP, that alone would yield $285 billion in budgetary savings—that is, more than half the amount needed to bring the structural deficit within the historic average of about of 2 percent of GDP.

As with health care, it may not be politically realistic to cut that much from the military budget. But even within the range of what Washington insiders consider realistic, the Pentagon should be able to target around $140 billion in annual savings.[6] This would still leave the military with a budget of nearly $600 billion, or 4 percent of GDP.

Taxing Wall Street. This would be a small sales tax on all financial transactions. The point of the tax would be to raise costs for short-term speculative traders while having a negligible impact on longer time-horizon "trade and hold" market participants. Variations of this proposal have floated through Congress for nearly 25 years. After the 1987 Wall Street crash, the idea was endorsed by both House Speaker Jim Wright, a Democrat, and Treasury Secretary Nicholas Brady, a Republican. Since the 2008–09 financial crisis and recession, support for the tax has been gaining momentum rapidly in the U.S. as well as Europe. Enacting such a tax has been a major focus of the Occupy Wall Street movement and has been supported effectively throughout the country by the organizing efforts of the National Nurses Union. The most recent proposal in Congress was introduced by Senator Tom Harkin and Representative Peter DeFazio in November 2011.

In its various incarnations, the tax rate proposed most frequently has been 0.5 percent for all stock sales. A viable tax structure could begin from this figure, along with a sliding scale on all other financial transactions. For example, the tax on a 50-year bond would be set as equal to the 0.5 percent rate on stocks, with the tax rates falling proportionally on bonds of shorter maturity (e.g. the tax rate on a 40-year bond would be 0.4 percent). Working within this framework, Dean Baker and I, along with colleagues, have estimated that this tax would raise approximately $350 billion per year if speculative trading did not decline at all after the tax was imposed (Pollin, Baker, and Schaberg 2003; Baker, Pollin, McArthur, and Sherman 2009). But even if trading declined by 50 percent as a result of the tax, the government would still raise about $175 billion annually. It would do so while also generating the additional benefit of discouraging excessive speculative trading on financial markets.[7]

Overall, if we take high-end figures for revenues generated by a financial transaction tax along with savings from health care and military spending cost controls, we can get well above the roughly $450 billion per year needed to bring the structural deficit into the range of two percent of GDP. But we can still achieve around $450 billion in total deficit reduction through much more modest assumptions about the generating revenue from a financial transaction tax and cost savings with health care and the military.

Could cuts in military and health care spending themselves create unemployment, just as the economy is rebounding from the recession? This is possible, if the recovery remains weak over the next 2–3 years. However, the most effective way to address this concern is not to maintain wasteful levels of military and health-care spending, but rather accelerate the transition to a clean-energy economy. As I have described above, clean energy investments generate, on a per-dollar basis, about 50 percent more jobs in the U.S. than military spending and three times more jobs than spending within the fossil fuels industry. This includes employment opportunities across all job categories and levels of educational credentials.[8]

Because of this, advancing the transition to a clean energy economy—among its many other benefits—can be the linchpin that connects the program for full employment with a progressive agenda for long-term deficit control.

6

If Not Now, When?

CREATING AN ECONOMY WITH AN ABUNDANCE of decent employment opportunities—a "full employment economy," as I have used the term—is a matter of basic ethics. Without full employment, the fundamental notion of equal rights for everyone—the core idea emanating from the Enlightenment and advanced further in both the liberal and socialist traditions—faces insurmountable obstacles in practical implementation. How can we claim that everyone in society has equal rights when those who are unemployed are not able to participate on a solid footing in the life of their community? The unemployed, as the historian Donald Sassoon has eloquently written, are rather preoccupied by "the needless worry of making ends meet, by the anger of being unwanted, unemployable, unacceptable, by the frustration of having become a human surplus which cannot be absorbed" (1996, p. 449).

Worse still, how can the unemployed feel that their rights are being respected when economic policymakers operate openly on the assumption that tens of millions of people need to remain unemployed or underemployed in order to prevent inflation from getting out of hand, as if these policymakers could pursue no other approaches for controlling inflation? These are the same policymakers who, in the aftermath of the financial collapse and Great Recession, have demonstrated true ingenuity in channeling unlimited amounts of money to commercial banks to keep them afloat, even while being unwilling to push those banks to use their freely obtained funds to create jobs, as opposed to holding massive cash hoards.

The United States economy is, of course, capitalist, which means that businesses operate to earn a profit, not to help reduce unemployment by hiring more workers than they need. But this is exactly the point: the U.S. economy is not just the sum of its individual business enterprises. These businesses function within a society that makes strong claims of supporting equal rights for all. At the very least, this should mean that we are committed to asking the hard question: Is it really impossible for a capitalist society, and the United States specifically, to find the appropriate combination of policies to reach full employment and stay there?

The central argument of this short book is that full employment is achievable in the United States today, even after we take full account of the many challenges involved. These include controlling inflation without stamping out job opportunities, counteracting the pressures created by the global reserve army of labor, respecting the environmental constraints on growth and reversing climate change, and, of course, transforming what has been an out-of-control financial casino into a vehicle for promoting productive investments, job creation, and environmental sustainability. By way of conclusion, it may be useful to consider these various challenges again, viewing them now through a wider lens and alternative vantage points.

The Green Agenda Will Create Jobs

I presented evidence on green investments and jobs in Chapter 5, but it is worth reviewing the matter again, since large numbers of people are either skeptical of such results or simply ignore them. The context is familiar: for most of the past generation, the aims of environmental sustainability and job creation have been seen as similarly worthy, yet painfully and unavoidably in conflict. "Jobs versus the environment" is frequently cited as a classic example of how public policy choices are fraught with trade-offs and unintended consequences—how you could end up doing harm while seeking to do good. Tree-huggers and spotted owls were pitted against loggers and hard-hats.

A recent round of this debate focused on the impacts of constructing the Keystone Pipeline, which was designed to carry tar sands oil from Alberta, Canada through the U.S. Midwest, delivering crude oil to refineries in Illinois, Oklahoma, and the Gulf Coast of Texas. Supporters of Keystone insisted that this would be a boon for job creation while opponents clamed both that the job benefits would be negligible while the environmental damage could be severe. As of this writing, President Obama has stopped the project from moving forward. Amid this debate, a Rasmussen Reports poll found that 59 percent of U.S. voters believe that creating new jobs is more important than environmental protection, and 29 percent held that protecting the environment is more important.

However, the key finding of my research is that there does not have to be any trade-off at all between jobs and the environment. Rather, investing at a large scale in energy efficiency—such as building retrofits, a "smart grid" electrical transmission system, and public transportation—and renewable energy—including wind, solar and geothermal power—can be a major new engine of job creation for a generation. The reason is simple, though it does not result from the intrinsic environmental benefits of these types of investments. The point is that making the necessary investments to build a clean energy economy requires roughly three times more people per dollar of expenditure than spending on producing and delivering coal, oil, and natural gas. As one example, the roughly $10 billion we would spend to retrofit 40,000 commercial buildings in the U.S. would produce three jobs for every one job created by spending the same amount of money to construct and operate the Keystone Pipeline, and to refine and deliver to consumers the oil that flowed through the pipeline. These job benefits would be in addition to building owners seeing their energy bills cut by about one-third and greenhouse gas emissions produced by these buildings also falling by one-third. In short, the transition to a clean energy economy has the capacity to merge the aims of environmental protection and economic justice to an unprecedented degree.

Connecting Short- and Long-run Goals

The recovery from the 2008–09 economic collapse has been slow and fitful. Moreover, as we have seen, even if the pace of recovery accelerates to equal the average rate of recent previous recoveries, the official unemployment rate would still not fall to five percent until early 2017 and to four percent until mid-2018. This is why the federal government needs to pursue further short-run stimulus policies as well as related measures to mobilize the cash hoards held by commercial banks, and similarly outsized liquid asset holdings by big corporations, into job-generating investments.

But the crisis for U.S. workers also did not begin in 2008. Conditions have been hard for working people in the United States for nearly 40 years as a result of neoliberal globalization. The clearest indicator of this is that average real wages in the U.S. have stagnated since the early 1970s while productivity has more than doubled. Ending the long-term dominance of neoliberal policies is therefore a must.

A basic step toward that end will entail transforming the economy's structure so that it can effectively counteract the pressures on workers resulting from globalization. This begins with significantly expanding investments in clean energy and education, and commensurately reducing spending on fossil fuel energy and the military. The impact of such a structural change—and specifically of reducing spending on fossil fuels and the military by 25 percent and moving all of those funds into clean energy and educational investments—will be to generate about 5 million more jobs.

This kind of structural transformation of the U.S. economy will not happen overnight. Nevertheless, we can begin to pursue this long-run agenda now, and in a manner that addresses short-term needs. For example, making investments today in raising the energy efficiency of our existing building stock is the fastest way to re-employ the two million construction workers who have lost their jobs since 2008. The federal government also needs to cover the huge budget gaps faced by state and local governments due to the recession. This will prevent, among other things, continued layoffs of teachers, school-bus drivers, and cafeteria workers. Precisely because clean energy and education investments are so central to expanding individual opportunity and protecting the environment, a stimulus program heavily weighted toward these priorities will be money effectively spent, in both the short and long runs.

Raising Job Quality Standards

Many pieces are needed to raise the overall quality of employment opportunities, including a national minimum wage set at the highest possible level without threatening to raise unemployment. This wage is probably around $12 per hour (in 2012 dollars). A $12 per hour minimum wage would substantially improve conditions for about 60 million working people and their families. This amounts to about 40 percent of the U.S. labor market, with well over half of these being either women or minorities.

However, the most effective means of raising job quality standards is sustained full employment itself. Under full employment, workers' bargaining power will rise. This was exactly Marx's point 160 years ago in his chapter on the reserve army of labor, and this was equally the lesson of the late 1990s, when wages rose sharply in the United States, especially for those at the lower end of the pay scale, as unemployment fell below 4 percent.

In a full employment economy, unions also gain increased leverage as representatives of workers' interests. Business owners typically employ, as needed, lawyers, accountants, public-relations firms, security guards, and scab laborers to enhance their bargaining strength, in addition to the leverage created by the reserve army outside the office or factory door. Working people deserve some effective countervailing representation. In short, full employment and effective unions are complimentary means, along with decent minimum wage laws, for achieving rising working- and middle-class living standards. This is especially true since, as the Swedish example shows, strong unions can play a central role in managing inflationary pressures in an economy committed to full employment.

Full Employment and the Welfare State

Sociologist Lane Kenworthy (2011) has shown that, between 1979 and 2007, 20 relatively rich countries, including the United States, frequently delivered decent work conditions and living standards to low-income people without achieving near-full employment. Following from these results, Kenworthy proposes expanding the Earned Income Tax Credit (EITC)—the U.S. government program that provides supplemental income for low-wage workers and their families—as a "back up" alternative to full employment.

I agree that making the EITC more generous is a highly desirable goal. But the benefits of an expanded EITC vary dramatically depending on the proportion of low-income workers who have full-time or nearly full-time jobs. This was made clear in recent research by my coworkers Jeannette Wicks-Lim and Jeff Thompson at the Political Economy Research Institute (2010). They measured the benefits to low-income families of a greatly expanded EITC along with a $12.30 minimum wage under the actual employment levels of 2005–2007. They then examined how much the benefits to families would increase if all low-wage workers with part-time jobs were raised to full-time. They show that raising all low-wage workers to full-time, combined with the EITC expansion and minimum wage increase, raises nearly four times more families above a basic-budget income line than the expansion of the EITC and rise in minimum wage implemented with all part-time workers remaining part-time. In short, an expanded EITC and similar measures should be seen as supplements to full employment, not as substitutes.

Globalization and Trade

I know many progressives oppose my contention that the United States can achieve full employment without having to reduce its trade deficit much below the current level of about 4 percent of GDP. Yet we don't need high-powered theories and statistics to resolve the issue, given that in the late 1990s, U.S. unemployment did already fall below 4 percent while operating with a trade deficit equivalent to the current level. There is also a more general issue at play. That is, most other countries, especially developing countries, benefit more from selling products in U.S. markets than the U.S. economy is harmed by running trade deficits at current levels. The U.S. dollar remains the world's most desirable currency, which enables the United States, uniquely, to continue importing more than it exports without having to undertake serious adjustments to close that gap. As I have discussed in Chapter 5, the United States should pursue industrial policies to promote innovation and growth in manufacturing, especially around clean energy and related environmental projects. But this does not mean it should be committed to expanding domestic job opportunities by reducing opportunities in, for example, Vietnam, Kenya, and Guatemala.

That said, it is also true that developing economies, especially large successful exporters such as China and India, should shift their growth strategies away from relying on exporting to rich countries. These countries should increasingly become focused on raising wages and improving working conditions among the still-overwhelming majority of poor people within their borders. This will lead to growing domestic markets in the developing world, enabling working people there to buy the products they themselves produce.

While this kind of domestically focused wage-led growth model for developing countries is compelling, it cannot be implemented overnight, even assuming the majority of policymakers in these countries embraced the approach. In the meantime, developing countries will continue to rely substantially on selling their products in U.S. markets. But this need not pose major difficulties within the United States precisely because we are capable of achieving full employment while maintaining a trade deficit at roughly the current level.

Governments, Markets, and Ethics

The measures I have proposed to build a full employment economy in the United States will entail substantial levels of government intervention. In considering such proposals, we must keep in mind the crucial truth which, at least rhetorically, is the starting point for most conservative economic pronouncements: that governments at all levels in the Unites States are often incompetent or corrupt in managing the economy.

However, what conservatives typically neglect is that government initiatives are frequently successful, sometimes emphatically so. Government programs in the United States have produced, among other things, a large number of outstanding public universities and a Social Security system that has succeeded in dramatically reducing poverty among the aged and disabled. I discussed in Chapter 5 the pathbreaking research by Vernon Ruttan, a leading authority on the economics of technological change. Ruttan has shown how the public sector has played "an important role in the research and technology development for almost every industry in which the United States was, in the late twentieth century, globally competitive" (2006, vii). Ruttan points to the aerospace, computer, and Internet industries as three epoch-defining cases.

Moreover, just as surely as government action has frequently been effective, markets do also regularly fail. The classic book *Manias, Panics, and Crashes* (1978) by Charles Kindleberger makes clear that, throughout the history of capitalism, unregulated financial markets have persistently produced instability and crises. Our most recent experience with financial deregulation delivering economic disaster was no aberration. We now also know—and even some conservatives will acknowledge—that protecting the environment and controlling climate change are challenges well beyond the capacity of even perfectly operating markets, much less the regularly mal-functioning variety that shape our everyday lives.

Creating decent employment opportunities for everyone—a full employment economy—is too fundamental a project to be left to the vagaries either of markets or governments. It is rather the task of an engaged citizenry to figure out how best to combine what is valuable both with markets and governments to create higher standards of well being, fairness, and ecology—i.e., a greater commitment to morality—throughout our society.

Notes

Chapter 1

[1] The patterns on inequality are surveyed well in MacEwan and Miller (2011), Chapter 3.

Chapter 2

[1] The two valuable discussions of the Meidner-Rehn model for Sweden are Erixxon (2010) and Marshall (1995).

[2] See the fascinating interview with Meidner (1998) in which he reflects on the successes and failures of the Swedish model.

[3] As Meidner himself wrote, "In the beginning of the 1990s—or to be exact in the government's budget proposal in January 1991—the Social Democratic government explicitly changed its

priorities. The main objective was shifted from full employment to price stability and the government announced its intention to apply for EU membership. The new non-socialist government which came into office in October 1991 allowed unemployment to rise steeply from 2–3 percent to more than 8 percent" (1997, p. 93).

Chapter 3

[1] Fuller's presentations on these themes are in Pollin (2003) Chapters 1–3 and Pollin (2007).

[2] An earlier and somewhat fuller version of this discussion is Pollin (2011a).

[3] See, among his other studies, Card (2005).

[4] DeFreitas (1998) surveys this evidence well.

[5] Frank Bardacke's masterful history of the United Farmworkers Union (2011) describes in depth the tragic conflicts that emerged between UFW organizers and undocumented Mexicans seeking work in the agricultural fields. As Bardacke shows, the UFW under César Chávez frequently took aggressive actions in the 1960s and 1970s to keep undocumented Mexicans out of the fields, and more generally out of the United States altogether. Chavez argued that this was necessary to prevent downward pressure on the decent wage standards that the UFW had fought hard to win for its members.

[6] This discussion draws from Pollin (2010a).

Chapter 4

[1] This discussion draws from Pollin (2010b).

[2] A fuller treatment of this issue is in Pollin (2012).

[3] See, for example, Federal Reserve researchers Maki and Columbo (2001).

[4] Detailed presentations for this section and the remainder of this chapter can be found in Pollin, Heintz, Garrett-Peltier, and Wicks-Lim (2011).

[5] These estimates are based on calculations by Mark Thoma reported on his blog, "Economist's View." Thoma found that during the previous three recoveries from recessions, the rate of reduction in unemployment from the low-point of the recession was 0.61 percentage points per month.

Chapter 5

[1] My coworkers at the Political Economy Research Institute and I developed the data, working directly from the industrial surveys and input-output tables of the U.S. Commerce Department. See, for example, Pollin and Garrett-Peltier (2011) for a methodological discussion and data on the employment effects of military versus domestic spending priorities. Pollin, Heintz, and Garrett-Peltier (2009) presents similar calculations that compare the employment effects of spending on clean energy investments with the effects of spending on fossil fuels.

[2] This discussion draws from Pollin (2010c).

[3] This section draws from Pollin (2011b). A fuller discussion is in Epstein and Pollin (2011).

[4] This discussion draws from Pollin (2012).

[5] A classic analysis of these issues is in Eisner (1986).

[6] See Pemberton and Korb (2011) on debate surrounding the U.S. military budget.

[7] See Pollin and Heintz (2011) for a detailed analysis of how the imposition of a financial transaction tax would affect market trading patterns in the United States.

[8] See Pollin and Garrett-Peltier (2011).

References

Baker, Dean, Robert Pollin, Travis McArthur, and Matt Sherman (2009) "The Potential Revenue from Financial Transaction Taxes," joint Working Paper from the Political Economy Research Institute and Center for Economic Policy Research, #212, http://www.peri.umass.edu/fileadmin/pdf/working_papers/working_papers_201-250/WP212.pdf

Bardacke, Frank (2011) *Trampling Out the Vintage: Cesar Chavez and the Two Souls of the United Farmworkers*, New York: Verso Press.

Blanchard, Oliver and Roberto Perotti (2002) "An Empirical Characterization of the Dynamic Effects of Changes in Government Spending and Taxes on Output," *Quarterly Journal of Economics* 117, no. 4, 1329–68.

Blinder, Alan (2006) "Offshoring: The Next Great Industrial Revolution?" *Foreign Affairs*, March-April.

Block, Fred (2008) "Swimming Against the Current: The Rise of a Hidden Developmental State in the United States," *Politics and Society*, 36:2, 169–206.

Card, David (2005) "Is the New Immigration Really So Bad?" *NBER Working Paper 11547* (August), Cambridge, MA: National Bureau of Economic Research.

Congressional Budget Office (2011b) *Long Term Budget Outlook*, June, Washington, D.C., http://cbo.gov/publication/41486

DeFreitas, Gregory (1998) "Immigration, Inequality, and Policy Alternatives," in Dean Baker, Gerald Epstein, and Robert Pollin, eds. *Globalization and Progressive Economic Policy*, New York: Cambridge University Press, 337–56.

Eisner, Robert (1986) *How Real is the Federal Deficit?* New York: The Free Press.

Epstein, Gerald and Robert Pollin (2011) "Regulating Wall Street: Exploring the Political Economy of the Possible," in Philip Arestis, Ed. *Microeconomics, Macroeconomics and Economic Policy: Essays in Honor of Malcolm Sawyer*, London: Palgrave Macmillan, 2011, 268–85.

Erixon, Lennart (2010) "The Rehn-Meidner model in Sweden: Its Rise, Challenges and Survival," *Journal of Economic Issues*, 44(3).

Feldstein, Martin. 2010. "Inflation or Deflation?" Project Syndicate, June 23, www.projectsyndicate.org/commentary/feldstein24/English

Friedman, Milton (1968) "The Role of Monetary Policy," *Ameri-*

can Economic Review (68:1), 1–17.

Ginsburg, Helen Lachs and Margurerite G. Rosenthal (2006) "The Ups and Downs of the Swedish Welfare State: General Trends, Benefits and Caregiving," *New Politics*, X1, 1, 1–11.

Glickman, Lawrence B. (1999) *A Living Wage: American Workers and the Making of Consumer Society*, Ithaca, NY: Cornell University Press.

Kalecki, Michal (1971) "Political Aspects of Full Employment," Ch. 12 of his *Selected Essays on the Dynamics of the Capitalist Economy*, Cambridge, U.K.: Cambridge University Press, 138–45.

Kenworthy, Lane (2011) *Progress for the Poor*, New York: Oxford University Press.

Keynes, John Maynard (1936) *The General Theory of Employment, Interest and Money*, London: Macmillan.

Kindleberger, Charles (1978) *Manias, Panics and Crashes: A History of Financial Crises*, New York: Basic Books.

MacEwan, Arthur and John Miller (2011) *Economic Collapse, Economic Change: Getting to the Roots of the Crisis*, Armonk, NY: M.E. Sharpe Publishers.

Maki, Dean M. and Michael G. Columbo (2001) "Disentangling the Wealth Effect: A Cohort Analysis of Household Saving in the 1990s," Washington, D.C.: Board of Governors of Federal Reserve System, http://www.federalreserve.gov/pubs/feds/2001/200121/200121pap.pdf

Marx, Karl (1967) *Capital, Volume I,* New York: International Publishers.

Marshall, Mike (1995) "Lessons from the Experience of the Swedish Model," in Philip Arestis and Mike Marshall, Eds., *The Political Economy of Full Employment,* Northampton, MA: Edward Elgar Publishers, Ch. 10.

Meidner, Rudolph (1997) "The Swedish Model in an Era of Mass Unemployment," *Economic and Industrial Democracy,* 18, 87–97.

Meidner, Rudolph (1998) "The Rise and Fall of the Swedish Model," (interview with Bertram Silverman), *Challenge,* January–February, 69–90.

Pemberton, Miriam and Lawrence Korb (2011) *A Report of the Task Force on a Unified Security Budget for the United States,* July, Washington, D.C.: Institute for Policy Studies.

Phillips, A.W. (1958) "The Relationship between Unemployment and the Rate of Change of Money Wage Rates in the United Kingdom," 1861–1957, *Economica,* New Series, 25:100, pp. 283–99.

Pollin, Robert (2003) *Contours of Descent: U.S. Economic Fractures and the Landscape of Global Austerity,* London: Verso.

Pollin, Robert (2007) "Global Outsourcing and the U.S. Working Class," *New Labor Forum,* 16(1): 122–25.

Pollin, Robert (2010a) "U.S. Trade Policy and the Jobs Crisis," *New Labor Forum,* 19(3): 82–5.

Pollin, Robert (2010b) "Austerity Is Not a Solution: Why the

Deficit Hawks Are Wrong," *Challenge* 53(6): 6–36.

Pollin, Robert (2010c) "Industrial Policy and the Revival of U.S. Manufacturing," *New Labor Forum*, 19:1, 58–61.

Pollin, Robert (2011a) "Can We Please Stop Blaming Immigrants?" *New Labor Forum* 20(1): 86–9.

Pollin, Robert (2011b) "Field Notes on Wall Street Reform: The Battle Continues," *New Labor Forum*, 20:2, 84–7.

Pollin, Robert (2012) "U.S. Government Deficits and Debt amid the Great Recession: What the Evidence Shows," *Cambridge Journal of Economics*, 36, 161–87.

Pollin, Robert, Dean Baker and Marc Schaberg (2003) "Securities Transaction Taxes for U.S. Financial Markets," *Eastern Economic Journal,* Fall, pp. 527–59.

Pollin, Robert and Heidi Garett-Peltier (2011) *The U.S. Employment Effects of Military and Domestic Spending Priorities: 2011 Update*, Amherst, MA: Political Economy Research Institute, http://www.peri.umass.edu/fileadmin/pdf/published_study/PERI_military_spending_2011.pdf

Pollin, Robert and James Heintz (2011) "Transaction Costs, Trading Elasticities, and the Revenue Potential of Financial Transaction Taxes for the United States," Amherst, MA: Political Economy Research Institue, PERI Research Brief, December, http://www.peri.umass.edu/fileadmin/pdf/research_brief/PERI_FTT_Research_Brief.pdf

Pollin, Robert, James Heintz, and Heidi Garrett-Peltier (2009)

The Economic Benefits of Investing in Clean Energy, Washington, D.C.: Center for American Progress.

Pollin, Robert, James Heintz, Heidi Garrett-Peltier and Jeannette Wicks-Lim (2011) *19 Million Jobs for U.S. Workers: The Impact of Channeling $1.4 Trillion in Excess Liquid Asset Holdings into Productive Investments*, Amherst, MA: Political Economy Research Institute, http://www.peri.umass.edu/fileadmin/pdf/published_study/PERI_19Million.pdf

Pollin, Robert and Jeannette Wicks-Lim. 2011. "Did Immigrants in the U.S. Labor Market Make Conditions Worse for Native Workers During the Great Recession?" PERI working paper no. 246. Amherst, MA: Political Economy Research Institute, http://www.peri.umass.edu/fileadmin/pdf/working_papers/working_papers_201-250/WP246.pdf

Ruttan, Vernon (2006) *Is War Necessary for Economic Growth? Military Procurement and Technology Development*, New York: Oxford University Press.

Sassoon, Donald (1996) *One Hundred Years of Socialism: The West European Left in the Twentieth Century*, New York: The New Press.

Stiglitz, J. (2010), *Freefall: America, Free Markets, and the Sinking of the World Economy*, paperback edition, New York: Norton.

Wicks-Lim, Jeannette and Jeffrey Thompson (2010) *Combining Minimum Wage and Earned Income Tax Credit Policies to Guarantee a Decent Living Standard to All U.S. Workers,* Amherst, MA: Political Economy Research Institute, http://www.peri.umass.edu/fileadmin/pdf/published_study/PERI_MW_EITC_Oct2010.pdf

Index

Griffin, Keith, 11–12

ABOUT THE AUTHOR

ROBERT POLLIN is Professor of Economics and Co-Director of the Political Economy Research Institute (PERI) at the University of Massachusetts-Amherst. His books include *Contours of Descent: U.S. Economic Fractures and the Landscape of Global Austerity* (2003); *An Employment-Targeted Economic Program for South Africa* (co-authored 2007); and *A Measure of Fairness: The Economics of Living Wages and Minimum Wages in the United States* (co-authored 2008). He has worked recently as a consultant for the U.S. Department of Energy, the International Labour Organization and numerous nongovernmental organizations on various aspects of building high-employment green economies, and is currently directing a project with the United Nations Industrial Development Organization on this topic. He has also directed projects on employment creation and poverty reduction in sub-Saharan Africa for the United Nations Development Program, and has been a member of the United States Competitive Policy Council. He is currently a member of the Scientific Advisory Committee of the European Commission project on Financialization, Economy, Society, and Sustainable Development.

BOSTON REVIEW BOOKS

Boston Review Books is an imprint of *Boston Review*, a bimonthly magazine of ideas. The book series, like the magazine, covers a lot of ground. But a few premises tie it all together: that democracy depends on public discussion; that sometimes understanding means going deep; that vast inequalities are unjust; and that human imagination breaks free from neat political categories. Visit bostonreview.net for more information.